the
declutter
workbook

the
declutter
workbook

101 feng shui steps to transform your life

mary lambert

STERLING PUBLISHING CO., INC.
NEW YORK

Published in 2004 by Sterling Publishing Co., Inc.
387 Park Avenue South, New York, NY 10016

First published in Great Britain in 2004 by
Cico Books
32 Great Sutton Street London EC1V 0NB

© 2004 Cico Books
Text © 2004 Mary Lambert

Distributed in Canada by Sterling Publishing
c/o Canadian Manda Group, One Atlantic Avenue
Suite 105, Toronto, Ontario, Canada M6K 3E7

Library of Congress Cataloging-in-Publication
Data available

1 0 9 8 7 6 5

ISBN 1–4027–1420–3

Editor: Liz Dean
Design: Paul Wood
Cover photograph: Geoff Dann
Illustrations: Trina Dalziel

Printed in Singapore

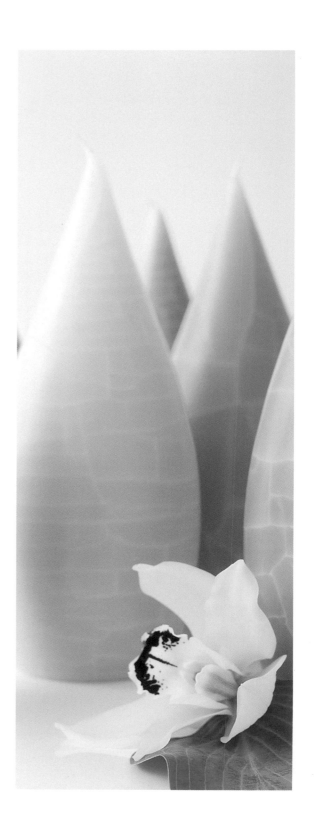

Contents

Introduction
Decluttering your world

Clearing out your home cleanses your life. As you release useless or old possessions that attach you to your past, you allow some space for desired items or opportunities to take their place. The Chinese art of feng shui has been implemented successfully since ancient times. The aim of feng shui is to promote a smooth flow of chi (energy) in the home, and to place furniture in the most auspicious positions. If piles of clutter are scattered about the home, they disrupt and slow down this energy flow, which over time can drain the health and wellbeing of the people living there. Clutter clearing is the first aspect of feng shui, and it is an incredibly powerful process – it literally brings amazing life changes.

CREATING A SHIFT

In my first book on dealing with junk, the bestselling *Clearing the Clutter*, I worked through the clutter hotspots in the different rooms in the home, suggesting how to clear them out and offering special storage solutions. In my second book, *Feng Shui Guide to Harmonious Living*, I took the clutter clearing a stage further. Here I talked about the disastrous effects of clutter accumulating in the eight feng shui aspirational areas of the home – depleting your finances in your Wealth space or affecting your relationship chances in your Marriage area – and introduced easy-to-perform purification ceremonies to cleanse and lift the atmosphere after a big clear-out.

The Declutter Workbook differs from the first two because it is entirely project-based — it's a hands-on, "doing" workbook. It takes you through all the rooms in your home, plus the yard or garden, and details specific clutter-clearing tasks to tackle — 101 in total. Every task is timed (look out for the calendar with the time at the start of each one) so that you can choose your tasks according to how much time you have. There are plenty of half-hour and hour-long tasks, so you can make an inroad into that clutter mountain even when your downtime is limited. You may want to start with sorting out your pictures in the hall, appraising your clothes in the bedroom, removing broken china in the kitchen, or cutting back overgrown shrubs in the yard — the choice is yours.

Clutter, as we all know, often creeps back, so maintenance timetables are included to help you monitor each area regularly. The last project deals with emotional decluttering — unique to *The Declutter Workbook* — because if you are storing clutter in your home, you need an emotional clearout, too. Feng shui practitioners believe practical clutter often mirrors mental clutter. A clear head and a clutter-free home go hand in hand.

We all need rewards for our efforts to dejunk our lives. So for every room you'll find a list of clearout treats — small items to buy for yourself — and a "wish card" to fill in (see page 96). Photocopy it on differently colored papers, and display it as you go through the transformation process. By writing down how you want your dream room to be, you take a step toward making it a reality.

Candles are wonderful energizers – use them in the living room and bathroom to lift the atmosphere.

MAKING A START

Clearing out your clutter can be overwhelming, so start with a small, hour-long project such as going through your kitchen's fridge/freezer (see page 16). Use my five-bag system to kickstart your de-junking. Keep plenty of big trash bags or boxes on hand, marking the first bag "Junk", the second bag "Thrift" or "Charity", the third bag "Things to be repaired or altered", the fourth bag "Things to sort and move", and the fifth bag "Transitional items" – these are belongings that you are not sure about. Put them in a cupboard for six months; get them out if you miss them, otherwise give them away. You may not use all of the bags, but you may need more for "Junk" and "Thrift".

YOUR SPECIAL TASKS

Toward the end of the book, there is a notebook section (see pages 66–92) where your drawing skills are needed. Questionnaires test you on your clutter overload in your home and yard or garden, and help you assess any emotional problems. Sample room plans highlight how typical energy flow is obstructed by clutter. Draw in all your rooms and your yard or garden to identify your major trouble spots.

After attacking the relevant tasks, and spending some time working on yourself, you will feel like a different person – liberated from useless clutter and emotionally revamped. Your world will embrace new challenges, and you'll gain a zest for living that you wouldn't have thought possible.

The softness of cushions makes them very yin, and ideal for the bedroom and living room.

The Hall Challenge

TO MAKE AN ENTRANCE: 5 HOURS

Step 1 – Complete the questionnaire
(see pages 68–69) and prepare yourself

Step 2 – Look at your entrance/hall

Step 3 – Clear the doorway

Step 4 – Sort your pictures

Step 5 – Review your mirrors

Step 6 – Search through junk mail and keys

Steps 7 & 8 – Your affirmation for success

STEP 1 GETTING STARTED

Fill in the questionnaire on pages 68–69 to assess your clutter problem. Do as much as you can cope with, but don't ever feel you haven't achieved enough. Locate your worst junk heaps, asking yourself questions such as:

● Can I easily open my front door?

● Do I have hoards of shoes and outdoor clothes lying in a heap?

● Are there always piles of old magazines and newspapers waiting to be removed?

Tackle the worst pile in each area first.

STEP 2 FOR AN INVITING ATMOSPHERE

Think about how it feels when you enter your home. Do you often feel irritated when you first come in? Are mountains of junk obstructing the entrance, so that it's always untidy and disordered? (Check your questionnaire answers.) Your entrance and hall welcomes people into your home, so these areas need to be vibrant and appealing. If chi (energy) can't enter easily, it slows down, creating a stifling atmosphere. Ask yourself if you are subliminally stopping people from visiting you. Write down how you want your hall to look.

STEP 3 THE DOORWAY

Check for:

✓ Shoes, boots

✓ Snow boots

✓ Jackets/coats, scarves, hats

✓ Strollers (pushchairs)

✓ Umbrellas (working and broken)

✓ Boxes of junk

✓ Bicycles, golf clubs

✓ Work bags/briefcases

This area can be a virtual dumping ground as the family come home and discards their items of the day. If it is not tackled straight away, people will feel pushed out by the disorder.

Get organized: Throw out obvious junk and broken objects; add more coatstands or closets for outdoor clothes; get a shoe tree/rack; ask for sports gear to be put away in relevant cupboards or the shed; store bikes in garage or shed; put work items neatly at side or in home office.

Maintenance: Spend ten minutes daily sorting out clutter that has crept back. Consider fining every household member a small amount for charity if they lapse into untidy habits.

Obvious benefits of clearout
You can easily open the door into a bright, clean hall.

Emotional benefits of clearout
A black cloud lifts from you mentally, you feel happier entering your home.

STEP 4 PICTURES
Check for:

✓ Holiday posters or enlarged photographs

✓ Female/male pictures

✓ Frightening abstracts or masks

✓ Sad, gloomy art

Study your hall pictures. Do you still like them? Our energy changes as we get older and so do our preferences – we all need new stimuli to represent the person we are becoming. If you're a single woman and have pictures everywhere of single women, you are saying that's the way you want to stay. If your pictures or masks are sad or frightening, what is that saying about your enjoyment of life? Posters or photos of a brilliant holiday have a short lifespan, so enjoy them for a while and then make a change.

Your hall should be an inviting place, free of clutter, that welcomes people in.

Obvious benefits of clearout
Your pictures get dusted and your walls cleaned as you move everything around.

Emotional benefits of clearout
You will feel much happier with inspiring pictures that depict what you like and want now.

Get organized: Discard old posters and photos; and offputting art; balance male/female art. Show pictures of happy couples to boost relationships or encourage them. Display recent photos.

Maintenance: Make minor changes every six months; bring in new art yearly.

STEP 5 MIRRORS

Check for:

✔ Cracked, discolored mirrors

✔ Mirrors that distort

✔ Mirrors propped up in the hall

✔ Mirrors facing the door

In feng shui, mirrors are very yang, or powerful, so use them sparingly. They can light up or expand halls, but if you display damaged mirrors, think about why you are trying to distort your vision of life.

Get organized: Discard damaged mirrors now; cover and store unused ones to prevent energy bouncing around. Clean a new mirror regularly so it reflects well. Never place a mirror opposite the front door (energy goes out again) or have two mirrors opposite each other – it creates energetic confusion.

Obvious benefits of clearout
A brighter, sparkling hall.

Emotional benefits of clearout
A positive energy-blast when you enter your home.

Maintenance: Check every six months for any cracks or signs of wear.

STEP 6 JUNK MAIL AND KEYS

Check for:

✔ Advertising leaflets, unopened credit card or charity envelopes, take-out menus, taxi cards

✔ Odd keys

The amount of mail that comes into our homes daily is phenomenal. Sticking it in a drawer or letting it pile up behind the door makes hidden piles of stale energy that will soon start to irritate you. And what about discarded keys from old locks, homes, or cars? Why do you want to hold on to items or places that are no longer a part of your life?

Get organized: Keep useful advertising, take-out leaflets, and taxi cards on a pinboard or in a folder. Discard the rest with unwanted charity or credit card information. Keep current keys and hang on hooks.

Obvious benefits of clearout
You can enter your home without tripping over a paper mound.

Emotional benefits of clearout
An ordered hall means an ordered mind.

Maintenance: Check leaflets weekly to stop the pile building again. When you have a new lock, car, home, or lockable item, dispense with old keys.

SUMMARY

Well done. Praise yourself for what you've achieved and see how good you feel. If you didn't manage to do all the tasks you wanted, just allocate some extra time to finish them.

Welcoming entrance

STEP 7 HALL REWARDS

Check for:

✓ Removing junk from the doorway

✓ Rationalizing your art

✓ Replacing broken mirrors

✓ Removing old junk mail and keys

This is an important area to keep clear, as this is where people get a first impression of your home. If you have managed at least two of the above goals, you are succeeding in de-junking this space. Allow yourself a couple of the treats below, or make your own choice.

Clearout treats

● A bunch of scented seasonal flowers for the hall table

● An attractive pinboard

● A bright rug that welcomes people in

● A new piece of art

● A new umbrella stand

● A mirror or a new picture light

STEP 8 YOUR WISH CARD

Before you finish your clearout, choose a photocopy of the card on page 96. Write down your wish for your ultimate hall, or choose one of the following.

"I choose a light and airy hall."

"I want a hall with pictures that lift my soul."

"I desire a hall that visitors love to enter."

"I would like a hall that is the delightful entrance to my sanctuary."

"I crave a hall with neat, ordered storage."

REAL-LIFE LETTING GO

I was working on the hall during a decluttering consultation in Patricia's apartment when I came across the junk drawer in her table there. As I rummaged through it, discarding notes and unused leaflets, I found a set of keys hidden at the back. When I showed them to Patricia, she looked a bit embarrassed as she admitted they were from a home that she had owned five years ago. She told me how she had found it hard to settle in her current home, and her keys were her way of hanging onto a loved property. I got her to throw out her old apartment keys, and a few weeks later she rang to say that she felt much more secure.

The Kitchen Challenge

FOR A ROOM OF NOURISHMENT: 5½ HOURS

Step 9 – Complete the questionnaire (see pages 68–69) and look at the kitchen

Step 10 – Cut back on seasonings, sauces, and spices

Step 11 – Hunt for unused appliances

Step 12 – Examine the contents of your fridge/freezer

Step 13 – Search through cupboards for any damaged china

Step 14 – Sort out the trash and unused plastic bags

Steps 15 & 16 – Your affirmation for success

STEP 9 MAKING A ROOM FOR HEALTHY EATING

Look around your kitchen. What are your feelings and first impressions about this room – is it the healthy, cozy haven it should be? (Check back on your answers to the questionnaire.) Or does it present a clutter disaster zone? Now ask yourself the following questions:

● Are your cupboards packed full of food or seasonings that are never used?

● Is there unknown food lurking in your fridge/freezer?

● Have you found unused appliances hidden away in corners?

● Are corners of your kitchen stuffed with old plastic bags or paper bags?

This is a room where food is prepared and eaten. It is the "heart" of the home, needing warmth and an agreeable atmosphere to draw in family and friends. If you feel depressed every time you enter this room, think why you are keeping it like this. Are you fearful of inviting people to share food with you? Now put down on paper what your special kitchen would be like.

STEP 10 SEASONINGS, SAUCES, AND SPICES

Check for:

✓ Rancid oils

✓ Old vinegars

✓ Stale spices and seasonings

✓ Sauces way past their best

✓ Stale cooking ingredients

Unfortunately, it can be very easy to keep cupboards full of ingredients that you use once or twice to make a special dish, and then they are rarely used again. And if all your seasonings and sauces are tightly packed in, those at the back can easily float past their use-by date without you realizing it. Spices in particular lose their pungency very quickly, so check on them frequently. Or, if you decant them into other

storage jars, note the last date to use them by. If you have kept too many old sauces and seasonings you lower the energy in this area, and symbolically say that you have lost your zest for life. So take the time now to plan a drastic clearout before you are affected by the dull energy levels.

Get organized: First, take everything out of the cupboard and work systematically through all the products, throwing out any past their use-by date. Trash old spices or those that have lost their pungency. Throw out old flours or dried-up raisins. Clean up any mess; place spices in racks behind doors, and sauces and seasonings in separate sections so that you can find them easily.

Obvious benefits of clearout

Cleaned-out cupboards with easy-to-find ingredients.

Emotional benefits of clearout

An energy boost after removing all those decaying items.

Maintenance: Assess your cupboards every three months and immediately throw out what's gone stale or rancid.

A kitchen needs to nurture you. Keep the surfaces and floor clear, and the cupboards full of healthy, fresh products.

STEP 11 UNUSED APPLIANCES

Check for:

✓ Unwanted gifts at the back of cupboards

✓ Equipment that no longer works

✓ Special-offer buys such as waffle makers or juicers that you may have forgotten about

Impressive-looking machinery that sits on the counter gathering dust or hiding at the back of a cupboard is taking up precious kitchen space. Equipment that you don't use, or which is broken beyond repair, is not adding to the productivity of this very positive area in the home. Let it go, allowing room for machinery that is wanted.

Get organized: Sell unwanted juicers or bread makers, or give to a friend who wants one; repair broken appliances or junk them.

Obvious benefits of clearout

Streamlined counters and tidier cupboards.

Emotional benefits of clearout

Relief that you now only have loved and functioning kitchen appliances.

Maintenance: Repair malfunctioning equipment immediately, or you never will. Check again every three to six months.

STEP 12 FRIDGE/FREEZER

Check for:

✓ Frozen meat, fish, or vegetables beyond their use-by-date

✓ Mystery bags of home-cooked food with freezer burn

✓ Abandoned condiment containers

✓ Dairy or similar products that have gone bad

✓ Rotting vegetables

A fridge/freezer represents the wealth and health of the family, so it should always be full of fresh and nourishing produce. Old, decaying, forgotten, or gungy foods represent a lack of concern for you or your family's welfare. Remove them immediately, and fill your fridge/freezer with food to entice the taste buds.

Get organized: Work through the fridge first. Eat up any leftovers within two days; remove any moldy food or suspect sauces, then clean out. Take any out-of-date meat, poultry, or vegetables from the freezer, wrap well, and throw away. Check for suspicious bags – dispense with anything unknown.

Obvious benefits of clearout

A clean and bacteria-free fridge/freezer.

Emotional benefits of clearout

A reassured feeling that you are safeguarding the family's health.

Maintenance: Have a quick check weekly; do a thorough investigation every two months.

Surround yourself with fresh vegetables to encourage good health in the family.

STEP 13 BROKEN AND DAMAGED CHINA

Check for:

✓ Chips and cracks on plates, bowls, and mugs, or cups

✓ Mismatched items

✓ Loose or broken handles on teapots and jugs

If the dishware that you use daily for all your meals is damaged in any way, you are pulling down the positive energy of the kitchen area and not looking after yourself or your family. Chipped pieces can also be unhygienic and encourage bacteria. Clear the way for some bright, modern pottery.

Get organized: Check through all china carefully – hairline cracks can be easily missed; throw out mismatched, chipped, or badly damaged items. Use invisible glue on any loved possessions that can be saved.

Obvious benefits of clearout

You are left with dishware that you are proud to use.

Emotional benefits of clearout

A lack of irritation as you set the table for meals.

Maintenance: Every time a serious chip appears, ditch the piece. Check thoroughly every three months.

Regularly buy some new modern crockery to replace damaged items.

STEP 14 TRASH CAN AND UNUSED BAGS

Check for:

✓ Overflowing trash – cans, fish, and chicken bones, vegetable peel, milk cartons

✓ A less-than-fresh aroma

✓ Bottles, newspapers, and plastic containers around the trash

✓ Plastic or paper bags, stuffed by the fridge or in cupboards

What does trash say to you? Things that are finished with, scraps, decaying matter, or empty containers –basically it's all dead energy. There is nothing positive about an overflowing bin – it is a dark space in your bright, sunny kitchen and needs controlling. Plastic bags always have a use, don't they? But if you keep hundreds, will you ever work through them all?

Get organized: Never overfill your trash; wrap left-over food well in newspaper; put newspapers, plastic, and glass bottles in your recycling bags or boxes. Re-employ a few plastic bags as liners for small pedal trash cans and ditch the rest. Keep a few for re-use.

Obvious benefits of clearout

A more orderly, sweet-smelling kitchen.

Emotional benefits of clearout

Your heart no longer sinks as you approach the trash area.

Maintenance: Empty the trash daily or every two days; keep only a few plastic or paper bags.

SUMMARY

Don't over-estimate what you can do. Praise yourself for what you have managed, and appreciate how welcoming your kitchen is becoming.

It's important to update all your kitchen equipment regularly to lift the energy.

Aromatic sanctuary

STEP 15 KITCHEN REWARDS

Check for:

✓ Clearing out your fridge/freezer

✓ Tackling your store cupboards

✓ Re-organizing your kitchen china

✓ Discarding plastic or paper bags and tackling the trash

✓ Letting go of dusty appliances

If you haven't gotten as far with your dejunking as you would like, but have managed to reach at least two of the above goals, it's time for one or two encouraging treats to make your kitchen area more inspiring. Buy from the following list or make your own selection, but take your time and acquire only what you really want.

Clearout treats

● Bright new mugs

● A patterned fruit bowl – keep it full of fruit to symbolize abundance

● A coffee pot and fresh coffee to awaken your senses

● Pots of fresh, pungent herbs for the windowsill

● Storage jars to fill up with dried beans, rice, flour, or other ingredients to show a healthy household

● Table mats and coasters to entice in dinner guests

STEP 16 YOUR WISH CARD

Before the end of your clearout, select a wish card from your photocopies of the card on page 96. Write down your wish for your perfect kitchen or choose one of the following:

"I crave a streamlined, ordered kitchen."

"I want a kitchen that all my family gathers in."

"I yearn for a kitchen that I love to cook in."

"My perfect kitchen always smells wonderful."

"I want a desirable kitchen full of healthy produce."

"I seek a stimulating kitchen where I can create wonderful meals."

REAL-LIFE LETTING GO

Unhappy with all her discarded appliances, Sarah decided to take them to a garage sale along with some other unwanted possessions. The appliances in particular sold very quickly for the prices she wanted, and Sarah made enough to buy the elaborate juicer she had been wanting for months.

The Living Room Challenge

FOR A ROOM OF RELAXATION: 12 HOURS

Step 17 – Complete the questionnaire (see pages 68–69) and study the living room

Step 18 – Be ruthless with photographs

Step 19 – Go through your bookshelves

Step 20 – Look at your music collection

Step 21– Root through your magazine rack

Step 22 – Check out your ornaments and decorations

Step 23 – Decide about damaged furniture

Step 24 – Appraise any inherited items

Steps 25 & 26 – Your affirmation for success

STEP 17 MAKING ROOM FOR SOCIABILITY

Stand in your living room door. Are you shocked by the mess you are viewing? (Check your answers to the questionnaire).

● Do you hoard photographs?

● Are books, magazines, CDs, and cassettes scattered everywhere?

● Is the room overloaded with ornaments and decorations, and/or broken or inherited pieces?

This is your room for unwinding and entertaining, so it needs to have an uplifting, convivial ambience. Ask yourself why you are making this room so uninviting; are you pushing your friends away? Write down a description of your dream living room.

STEP 18 PHOTOGRAPHS AND ALBUMS

Check for:

✓ Out-of-focus shots

✓ Photographs of people you have forgotten or no longer see

✓ Too many pictures of ex-partners

Decluttering your collection can be tough because photos remind you of the good times – but having heaps of them lying around in piles keeps you too attached to your past. They connect you to the person you once were, rather than who you are now, and also to people who are no longer important to you.

Get organized: Throw out unwanted shots – weed out excess pictures of ex-partners, people you no longer see, or people you dislike. Store loved photos in albums or index systems rather than in piles or bundles. Frame some current pictures that you really like.

Obvious benefits of clearout
Those irritating piles of photos have now gone from shelves or drawers.

Emotional benefits of clearout
You cut the ties with people you don't need in your life.

Maintenance: Every six months, make it a priority to check through any new photos you've accumulated. If you take digital pictures, delete bad or unwanted shots as you go.

STEP 19 BOOKSHELVES

Check for:

✓ Holiday fiction

   ✓ Dusty, out-of-date reference books

   ✓ Fading classics, not read for years

   ✓ Old travel books

It may seem prestigious to have a massive collection of books, but if they are hardly ever read, you felt obliged to take them from a relative, or they are just gathering dust, again they just link you to your past and old ideals. You need to allow space to bring in some new, stimulating books or knowledge that will advance you.

Get organized: Sort through your books a shelf at a time. Take unwanted paperbacks or classics to thrift (charity) stores, hospitals or libraries; junk old or out-of-date reference or travel books.

Keep the living room clutter-free and fill with plants and flowers for an embracing atmosphere.

Obvious benefits of clearout
You see gaps in your once overloaded bookshelves.

Emotional benefits of clearout
A feeling of letting go as you release books you no longer need.

Maintenance: Check every six months for paperbacks that have accumulated; audit any other titles yearly.

STEP 20 MUSIC COLLECTION

Check for:

✓ Discarded LPs

✓ Broken or warped cassettes

✓ Unwanted CDs

Your music collection should comprise albums that you really love and to which you regularly listen. As your body's energy changes over the years, so does your musical taste. You can hang on to some of your favorite old-time greats, but otherwise prepare yourself to let go of sentiment as you discard the music that you too have really outgrown.

Get organized: If you no longer have a record player, sell or give away all your old LPs and replace your favorites with the CD version; sort through, and throw out, any broken or poor-quality cassettes; pass on any CDs no longer played to friends, family or charity stores. Buy a new set of storage racks for your pared-down collection; store the albums you want to keep in alphabetical or category order for easy reference or access.

Obvious benefits of clearout
You can find all the albums that you want to play, and your living room floor is clear of music-related clutter.

Emotional benefits of clearout
After some initial sadness, you feel pleased that you now have only the music you really love and want to listen to.

Maintenance: Go through your collection yearly; if you buy albums regularly, investigate your music every six months.

STEP 21 MAGAZINE RACKS

Check for:

✓ Old holiday brochures

✓ Local magazines or newspapers from months ago

✓ Daily newspapers more than a week old

✓ Monthly magazines from a year back

✓ Any out-of-date catalogs

A bulging magazine rack will depress you every time you look at it – it creates a black "energy hole" in your living room. Do you cling to outdated fashion and designs catalogs, last season's holiday brochures or newspapers? If so, ask yourself why you feel the need to hang onto past news, travel or events long gone. Are you afraid of living in the present?

Get organized: Keep only your current holiday brochures; cut out any interesting magazine or newspaper articles for filing. Hang on to current catalogs and let go of the rest. Bundle up and throw away everything you can't recycle.

Obvious benefits of clearout
A magazine rack full of current reading material that stimulates you.

Emotional benefits of clearout
You no longer have that nagging voice in your head telling you to sort this area out.

Maintenance: Go through the magazine rack each month to keep on top of the paper mound.

STEP 22 DAMAGED FURNITURE

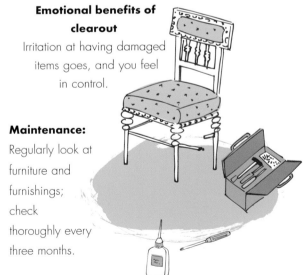

Check for:

✓ Scratched tables

✓ Sofas with torn upholstery

✓ Dining chairs with wobbly legs

✓ Cushions with broken zippers

If your furniture looks neglected, what does that say about you and how you are leading your life? Any damaged items will pull down the overall energy flow in your home, so repair any pieces or junk them.

Get organized: Fill scratches and revarnish tables or get professional help; cover torn upholstery with a throw; re-glue or nail wobbly chairs or dump them. Throw out broken cushion covers and buy some colorful new ones.

Obvious benefits of clearout
Repaired furniture and re-vamped furnishings add a new vibrancy to the room.

Emotional benefits of clearout
Irritation at having damaged items goes, and you feel in control.

Maintenance:
Regularly look at furniture and furnishings; check thoroughly every three months.

Surround yourself with well-maintained furniture that you adore.

STEP 23 DECORATIONS

Check for:

✔ Unwanted gifts from friends and relations

✔ Holiday mementoes that no longer appeal

✔ Presents from past partners

Decorations and ornaments can be a prominent feature in the living room, so they need to give you good, positive vibes. Don't buy into the stock answer, "I have to keep it, it was a present from a relative." You have to love all the pieces you keep. If anything is affecting you negatively every time you look at it, such as a statue given to you by an ex-partner, it just has to go.

Get organized: Look at all ornaments and decorations with a critical eye and put to one side anything you dislike. Give away any item that brings up bad emotions about the person who gave it; some holiday mementoes soon lose their appeal, so pass them on.

Obvious benefits of clearout

Space has appeared on your mantel and shelves.

Emotional benefits of clearout

You are now surrounded by possessions that you truly love.

Maintenance: Review your decorations every six months, and regularly reposition them for a positive energy shift.

STEP 24 INHERITED ITEMS

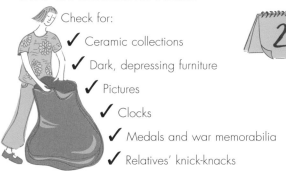

Check for:

✔ Ceramic collections

✔ Dark, depressing furniture

✔ Pictures

✔ Clocks

✔ Medals and war memorabilia

✔ Relatives' knick-knacks

The emotion we attach to inherited possessions is amazing – we feel that person imbued in them, but preserving items from dead loved ones can create a mausoleum of mis-matched belongings. It is a tough one, but if the inherited pieces have no place in your decor, let them go. Remember they match the energies of the person who owned them, not yours.

Get organized: Keep only what you love – you will always remember that person; junk worthless mementoes. Sell collections, clocks, and furniture; make a remembrance collage of favorite old photos – ditch the rest; keep or frame one or two medals or memorabilia, then sell or give the rest to a war museum.

Obvious benefits of clearout

Your living room regains your chosen style.

Emotional benefits of clearout

A wonderful feeling of letting go of the past.

Maintenance: Review every time belongings are passed on to you.

SUMMARY

Give yourself a pat on the back; your living room is unrecognizable from the start of your de-junking.

Sociable haven

STEP 25 LIVING ROOM REWARDS

Check for:

✓ Going through your photos

✓ Cutting down your book collection

✓ Disposing of unwanted music

✓ Trashing old magazines and newspapers

✓ Renovating furniture and furnishings

✓ Letting go of relatives' belongings

✓ Relinquishing some ornaments and decorations

How much have you done? If you have worked through at least four, ideally five, of the above goals, you are sorting out your clutter well and need a small treat to enhance your cleared-out living room. Choose from the following or make your own selection.

Clearout treats

● A metal or wooden picture frame

● Healthy, round-leaf plants or flowers to encourage more growth

● Some incense, such as basil, jasmine, or patchouli to promote good feelings

● A new book or CD you have really wanted for some time

● Pebbles, or a glass, or ceramic ornament for some grounding energy

● A rug that will enhance your decor

STEP 26 YOUR WISH CARD

Before you finish your clearout, take a wish card from your photocopies of the card on page 96. Write down a wish for your special living room from the following, or make one of your own.

"I want my living room to be warm and inviting."

"I need a living room that is calming and soothing."

"I long for my living room to be minimalist."

"My aim is to create a living room full of laughter and joy."

"I am making my living room a happy and pleasant family room."

"My dream living room is full of sociable people."

REAL-LIFE LETTING GO

Peter, a writer, loved his collection of books. But there were too many and they overcrowded his living room. He was reluctant to let go of some old paperbacks, but agreed he wanted space for new literature, and let them go. A few weeks later, he was offered a book deal from the same paperback publisher – he had let new opportunities come in.

The Bedroom Challenge

FOR A ROOM THAT CALMS: 7 HOURS

Step 27 – Complete the questionnaire (see pages 68–69) and study the bedroom

Step 28 – Look at the laundry

Step 29 – Check out the bed

Step 30 – Organize your clothes

Step 31 – Cut down on your shoes

Step 32 – Work through your cosmetics

Steps 33 & 34 – Your affirmation for success

STEP 27 MAKING A ROOM FOR BLISSFUL SLEEP

Stand at your bedroom door. Do you feel your heart sink as you view the existing disorder? (Check your answers to the questionnaire.)

● Are there boxes bulging with clothes and is junk teetering on top of your closets?

● Is the space under your bed a secret hideout for broken or unwanted items, or discarded clothes?

● Do you find that it's difficult to find your favorite perfume because it is always buried under mounds of useless clutter?

This is your resting room, so it needs a calm, embracing atmosphere in order to encourage peaceful sleep. Ask yourself if the disorder here reflects some other confusion in your life. Now note down what your blissful bedroom would ideally be like.

STEP 28 THE LAUNDRY BASKET

Check for:

✓ Overflowing basket

✓ Discarded items

✓ Piles of clothes scattered around the room

A full laundry basket creates a stagnant space in the bedroom, slowing down energy flow. Clothes pick up the negative vibrations of a normal working day – traveling stress, office trauma, and any upsets with children. Random clothes piles create a gridlock of stale energy. If you don't get down to tackling the clutter mountains, your mood can be adversely affected by the mess.

Get organized: Start by moving the laundry basket into the bathroom or the utility room; hang up clothes each night – even when you get home late, never leave garments hanging over a chair or littering the floor.

Obvious benefits of clearout

The room and floor look tidier and you can vacuum more easily.

Emotional benefits of clearout

Your mood lightens as you are no longer annoyed by scattered or piled-up clothes around the room.

Maintenance: Wash clothes every couple of days to avoid any build-up.

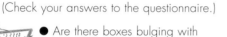

STEP 29 THE BED

Check for:

✔ Broken equipment, dirty clothes, old shoes, junk under bed

✔ Age of mattress

✔ Age of bed linen and duvet covers

A bed can store people's energies. If you are in a new relationship but still sleep in the bed that a long-term partner shared, you have not broken the tie with that person. Junk under the bed can disturb sleep or take the zing out of your sex life.

Get organized: Buy a new bed or mattress, or at least new bed linen; clear out the area under the bed, throw away junk, and store what you keep in closets or drawers.

Obvious benefits of clearout

You get a firm new bed or mattress to sleep on, or bright new bed linen.

Emotional benefits of clearout

A new bed or linen means a new start. You will sleep better with your new partner.

Maintenance: Make one of the above changes when a long-term relationship ends.

STEP 30 CLOTHES

Check for:

✔ Clothes not worn for a year

✔ Out-of-shape, delicate, or itchy dresses

✔ Too tight or old-fashioned pants/jackets/shirts

Renew your bed linen regularly, particularly if a relationship ends.

✔ Outdated, jokey T-shirts

✔ Unworn business suits

✔ Worn coats/outdoor wear

✔ Torn clothes/broken zippers

Most of us wear only twenty per cent of the clothes that we possess. Ask yourself why you are hanging onto things that no longer fit – why not buy clothes to flatter the current you? Clinging onto old items keeps you tied to your past image. Be ruthless: lay everything on the bed, and bring in a friend as an arbitrator to say what looks good on you.

Get organized: junk old, unworn, jokey or disliked items; repair damaged clothes; buy multiple hangers; keep sweaters/T shirts in clear plastic boxes; put work clothes at front and casual clothes at the back of the closet for easy access; place bags on large hooks.

Obvious benefits of clearout

Everything fits in your wardrobe.

Emotional benefits of clearout

You look good – and your self-esteem rockets

Maintenance: Review every season; when you buy something new, get rid of something old.

Maintenance: Check seasonally, and remember if you buy a new pair of shoes, try to get rid of some old ones.

STEP 32 COSMETICS

Check for:

✓ Worn-down lipsticks, eyeliner pencils, ratty brushes

✓ Messy or dried-up foundations, moisturizers, lip gloss, mascara, nail polish

✓ Eye shadows or blushers in unfashionable shades

Your make-up enhances the person you are today, not a few years ago, so it needs to be loved and up-to-date, and complement your clothes.

Get organized: Junk ancient messy make-up and brushes; throw away past season's eye shadows; keep only make-up used now; clean your make-up bag; store in clear plastic boxes.

Obvious benefits of clearout

You can quickly find that favorite lipstick or pencil.

Emotional benefits of clearout

You look and feel good.

Maintenance: Check every three months.

SUMMARY

Take a break – you have achieved a lot. Your bedroom is emerging as a much more inviting place to sleep.

STEP 31 SHOES

Check for:

✓ Shoes/boots with broken heels

✓ Old-fashioned styles

✓ Too-tight shoes or heels

✓ Unworn impulse buys

Shoes keep us grounded in life, so they need to be supportive and comfortable so that we feel good about ourselves. If your closet is full of shoes that are broken, ones that torture you or fashion-victim styles hardly worn, you are affecting your overall wellbeing.

Get organized: Pull shoes out, try them on, discard ones that are broken, uncomfortable, too high, or tight. Pass on to friends unworn or disliked styles. Store favorites neatly in pairs on racks.

Obvious benefits of clearout

You can now see the bottom of your closet.

Emotional benefits of clearout

You feel good wearing the shoes you love.

Bedded bliss

STEP 33 BEDROOM REWARDS

Check for:

✓ Sorting out the laundry basket

✓ Reviewing your bed

✓ Re-organizing your clothes and shoes

✓ Paring down your cosmetics

If you are well on your way to achieving a minimalist bedroom, and have achieved at least two of the above goals, you are doing well. So choose a couple of the treats below, or make your own choice, but remember plants or water features are not suitable for the bedroom (in feng shui they are wonderful energizers, whereas in this room you need tranquility).

STEP 34 YOUR WISH CARD

Just before you finish your clearout, take one of your photocopies of the card on page 96. Note down your wish for your special bedroom, or select one of the following.

"I need my bedroom to comfort and protect me."

"I yearn to have restful and restorative sleep in my bedroom."

"I long for peace and tranquility in my bedroom."

"I crave my bedroom to be sensuous and loving."

"I am ready for a passionate, alluring bedroom."

Clearout treats:

● A large lavender-scented candle

● An inspiring picture to hang opposite the bed

● A loving rose quartz crystal to go on your nightstand

● Cushions in a tactile material, such as velvet or satin

● An essential oil burner and some enticing ylang-ylang or rose essential oil

● A dreamcatcher to put over the bed to protect your dreams

If you choose the candle or aromatherapy oil burner, always extinguish the flame before sleep for safety reasons.

REAL-LIFE LETTING GO

Susan had been sleeping badly for a while and asked for my advice. On checking her bedroom, I found that her underbed area had become her dumping ground. It was littered with old shoes, discarded clothes, magazines, cat's toys, and a broken hairdryer. She threw the junk in the trash and vacuumed the area. She collapsed in bed that night, exhausted – and had her best night's sleep in many months.

The Child's Bedroom Challenge

FOR A ROOM OF REST AND STIMULATION: 5½ HOURS

Step 35 – Complete the questionnaire (see pages 68–69) and assess your child's bedroom

Step 36 – Look at the toy box

Step 37 – Go through all clothes and shoes

Step 38 – Sort out the underbed area

Step 39 – Check for current sports equipment

Steps 40 & 41 – Your affirmation for success

STEP 35 MAKING A ROOM FOR REST AND CREATIVITY

Study your child's room with a critical eye. Do you avoid going in there because of the existing chaos? (Check your answers to the questionnaire.)

● Are clothes scattered everywhere and falling out of the closets?

● Do you keep tripping over discarded toys?

● Have you spotted worn out racquets, bats, and balls threatening to break out from the closet – or unbelievable objects lurking under the bed?

A child's bedroom is a mixture of rest and play. It is here that he or she plays games, listens to music with friends, does homework, and finally drifts to sleep, so this room needs more of an uplifting atmosphere. If the room is overly cluttered, your child may be lethargic or sleep badly, or his/her school work may suffer. Write down how you think you can transform this room.

STEP 36 TOY BOX

Check for:

✔ Broken model cars, toy trucks, and trains

✔ Dolls with limbs missing; punctured balls, torn teddies or other soft toys

✔ Discarded toys that are linked to an old TV series

✔ Unread reading books or picture books, or those with ripped-out pages

Make sure that you child's underbed area is junk-free; only store bed linen here.

Young children have short attention spans. They happily play with a toy, lose interest or break it, and move on to something else. If their toy box is stuffed full of unused, broken or dismembered toys, rather than loved ones, this creates a low-energy space.

Get organized: Pull out all the broken toys, torn books and junk; give away character toys – other children may still like them. Take unwanted books to hospitals or libraries. Get more toy boxes, if needed, for loved toys – put the boxes on rollers so kids can easily pull out play items.

Obvious benefits of clearout

Bringing some order to this messy box.

Emotional benefits of clearout

Feelgood factor at giving toys to a deserving cause.

Maintenance: Check after every birthday and after Christmas each year.

STEP 37 CLOTHES AND SHOES

Check for:

✓ A tail of clothes around the room

✓ Outgrown dresses, pants, jumpers, baby clothes, shirts, T-shirts, and shoes

✓ Children's uncool clothing rejects

✓ Faded and frayed jackets and coats

Kids grow out of clothes fast, and if they are unworn they are cluttering up useful closet space. Clothes left on the floor carry the negative energies of the day, and need to be hung up or put in the laundry basket. Rejected or disliked clothing gives off bad vibrations in the closet.

Get organized: Install a laundry basket for dirty clothes; pass on outgrown or rejected clothes and shoes to friends' children or to charity. Dispense with worn-out, frayed clothing. Sort clothing into school and leisure wear; fit shoe racks and add shelving for sweaters, shirts, and T-shirts.

Obvious benefits of clearout

Organized wardrobes and a tidier bedroom.

Emotional benefits of clearout

You're happy that your child has a better environment for sleep and play.

Maintenance: Take a look every six months; every three months if your child is growing rapidly.

STEP 38 UNDER THE BED

Check for:

✓ Discarded pajamas, socks, screwed-up clothes, shoes, and sneakers

✓ Candy wrappers, half-eaten food, soda cans

✓ Abandoned games, half-finished puzzles, lost toys

✓ Computer games, disks, crayons, pencils, and scraps of paper

Losing sundry items under the bed is a common habit for both adults and children. But growing children can be more vulnerable to this stale pile of energy lingering beneath them when they are resting. It can cause erratic or disturbed sleep, and affect their concentration in everything they do. Make this a forbidden zone for junk.

Get organized: Throw out trash; wash dirty clothes; tidy away shoes. Store games and puzzles in a closet; put toys back in box. Place computer games and disks in neat racks and writing equipment in stationery holders. Clean well and keep nothing under the bed, or only some current clothes or linen in a pull-out drawer.

Obvious benefits of clearout

A spotless area under the bed.

Emotional benefits of clearout

You feel thankful that your child's room is now more conducive to sleep.

Maintenance: Patrol this area regularly – every two or three days.

STEP 39 SPORTS EQUIPMENT

Check for:

✓ Deflated soccer/rugby balls, old tennis balls, broken rackets, table tennis bats, baseball bats and mitts, abandoned skateboards, and frisbees

✓ Untouchable sneakers

Hoarding old unused sports equipment is just keeping your child linked to activities he or she no longer enjoys, or to an item he has long outgrown. Surround him with his current sporting loves.

Get organized: Throw away any damaged equipment; give rejects to friends or sports clubs. Store the remainder neatly in a designated section of the closet for easy retrieval.

Obvious benefits of clearout

No more danger zones – abandoned equipment won't assault you as it falls out of the closet.

Emotional benefits of clearout

A contented child with sports gear that he or she uses often.

Maintenance: Look at equipment yearly, or every six months for a sports fiend.

SUMMARY

Take few deep breaths. You have tackled some tricky projects – especially if you've taken on an older child's bedroom. If you lost a few battles, think about convincing your child to clean in a different way.

A Restful Den

STEP 40 CHILD'S BEDROOM REWARDS

Check for:

✓ Sorting out the toy box

✓ Dejunking under the bed

✓ Streamlining sports equipment

✓ Updating clothes and shoes

This area is harder to declutter as it is more out of your control, but if you have achieved at least two of these goals, you deserve to buy one or two treats to make this tidier space more appealing. Select from the following, or choose your own treat.

Clearout treats:

● A fabric laundry sack

● Brightly colored or transparent plastic toy boxes

● An amethyst crystal – put by the bed of an older child to balance their emotions

● A lamp for night-time reading

● A poster that your child loves

● A big cushion or beanbag for play and relaxation

STEP 41 YOUR WISH CARD

Before your clearout ends, take a wish card from your photocopies of the card on page 96. Write down your own wish for your ordered child's bedroom, or put down one of the following:

"I desire my child's bedroom to be a restful sanctuary."

"I seek peace and order in my child's bedroom."

"I want my child to sleep contentedly in her bedroom."

"I yearn for my child to have a tidy bedroom."

"I long for my child's bedroom to be full of happiness."

"My child's bedroom will have a harmonious atmosphere."

REAL-LIFE LETTING GO

A client's daughter, Alison, was very attached to all her dolls but because she had so many, there wasn't room for all of them. After some persuading, she put her favorites to one side and allowed her mother to take the rest to a children's home. She felt a warm glow when her mother told her how happy the children were with their new playthings.

The Bathroom Challenge

FOR A ROOM THAT SOOTHES: 5¼ HOURS

Step 42 – Complete the questionnaire (see pages 68–69) and assess the bathroom

Step 43 – Inspect your towels and mats

Step 44 – Get rid of those beauty samples

Step 45 – Eliminate ex-partner's toiletries

Step 46 – Streamline your medicine cabinet

Step 47 – Take a look at your holiday treasures

Steps 48 & 49 Your affirmation for success

STEP 42 MAKING A ROOM FOR RECUPERATION

What do you feel about your bathroom when you step inside? Look around and detect 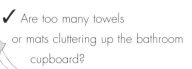 any hot spots of disorder (check your answers to the questionnaire).

✔ Are too many towels or mats cluttering up the bathroom cupboard?

✔ Are your cabinets clogged up with old medicines, piles of beauty samples, or old toiletries?

✔ Have your holiday treasures set around the tub lost their sparkle?

Your bathroom can be a wonderful haven where you soak away the cares of the day. If it is an utter mess, think about why you are denying yourself the relaxation you deserve. Energy moves slowly in the bathroom (water is always draining here, making the room yin, or passive) so clutter here hinders the flow even further – and slows you up. Now write down how you see your ultimate bathroom.

STEP 43 TOWELS AND MATS

Check for:

✔ Stiff, torn, or frayed towels

✔ Garish embroidered or named gift towels

✔ Balding or faded mats

Towels should be fluffy and luxurious. If most of yours are in bad condition, you are denying yourself the comfort you deserve. Mats literally help you to keep your feet on the ground; if you're still using ones that are worn or threadbare, your standing in life is undermined.

Get organized: Weed out the worst towels or mats and dispose of them. Give away disliked gift towels – they may be to someone else's taste. Sort the rest by size with favorites and newest styles on top and mats beneath.

Obvious benefits of clearout

You no longer have to use towels that scratch or have lost their fluffiness.

Emotional benefits of clearout

You feel more nurtured and secure.

Maintenance: Look at your towels and mats every few months; visit the sales for towel bargains.

Store your bathroom products neatly in units or containers to let the energy flow freely.

STEP 44 BEAUTY SAMPLES

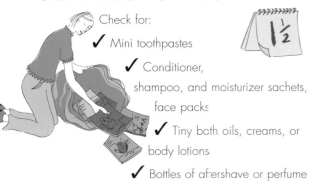

Check for:

✓ Mini toothpastes

✓ Conditioner, shampoo, and moisturizer sachets, face packs

✓ Tiny bath oils, creams, or body lotions

✓ Bottles of aftershave or perfume

Beauty samples come through the door all the time. They lodge themselves in the bathroom, and at first they are welcomed because they are free. If you love samples, you will probably use them in the first couple of weeks. Otherwise, they fester and eat up room in your cabinets – until you have a major clearout.

Get organized: Samples are great, but just display prominently those you want as a reminder to use them – and lose the rest. Put some in your gym bag, or travel light with them on weekend getaways.

Obvious benefits of clearout

More room for your favorite items.

Emotional benefits of clearout

You feel in control once more.

Maintenance: Keep useful samples; trash others.

STEP 45 EX-PARTNER'S TOILETRIES

Check for:

✓ Bottles of aftershaves and perfume/cologne

✓ Toothpaste, toothbrush, mouthwash

✓ Disposable razors, shaving foam

✓ Deodorant, make-up remover, and moisturizer

✓ Shampoo and conditioner

If your bathroom is full of products your ex-partner left behind, you are creating a shrine to them and will find it even harder to let go of your love. Be easy on yourself; cut the ties on a day when you are strong.

Get organized: Search for any toiletries belonging to your ex and get them out of your home; clean the room thoroughly.

Obvious benefits of clearout

More space for pampering products for you.

Emotional benefits of clearout

That relationship is history – you're living in the now.

Maintenance: Be strong – vow to throw out or return all of your ex-partner's grooming products whenever a relationship ends.

STEP 46 OLD MEDICINES

Check for:

✔ Bandaids that have lost their adhesion

✔ Skin creams, ointments, or lotions that are no longer effective

✔ Out-of-date pills, such as antiobiotics

✔ Grungy, half-finished bottles of cough mixture or sticky cough drops

✔ Ancient eye drops or contact lens solution

A medicine cabinet is linked to the health of the family and should be full of only current, prescribed remedies for ailments. Old medicines past their sell-by date encourage an atmosphere of ill health and can pull down the positive bathroom vibrations.

Get organized: Pick out anything that is out of date or unusable and throw away; return old antibiotics to a drug store/chemist. Get rid of half-finished grungy creams, ointments, and cough medicines. Re-plan your cabinet, drawers, or baskets to hold similar products together such as bandages and antiseptics.

Obvious benefits of clearout

It's faster to find the medicine you're seeking.

Emotional benefits of clearout

You feel better as all these old health products leave your home.

Maintenance: Your health is important, so don't keep medicine dregs. Check the validity of medications every three months.

STEP 47 VACATION TREASURES

Check for:

✔ Precious shells, pebbles, star fish

✔ Natural sponges

✔ Pieces of driftwood, feathers

Many of us love to decorate our bathrooms with natural vacation souvenirs, particularly shells. Rather than holding the memory of the good times in our heads we want a tangible possession. But vacations come and go, and so should these pieces when they are past their best.

Get organized: Get rid of dusty or rotting mementoes that now irritate you. Replace with current vacation finds.

Obvious benefits of clearout

You have fewer items to clean.

Emotional benefits of clearout

Releasing old attachments.

Maintenance: Renew your treasures regularly. Keep only what you love, and reappraise after each trip.

SUMMARY

Well that wasn't so bad, was it? You are well on the way to having the bathroom you want. Allocate more time to deal with any black spots.

Welcome retreat

STEP 48 BATHROOM REWARDS

Check for:

✓ Rationalizing beauty samples

✓ Being realistic about vacation treasures

✓ Updating your towels and mats

✓ Cutting back your medicinal supplies

✓ Trashing your ex-partner's bathroom goods

This is an important room to get right, but it takes time. If you have ticked off at least two goals above you are progressing well, and can allow yourself some treats to add to the ambience of this evolving room. Pick from the list below, or choose your own.

Clearout treats

● Geranium or marjoram essential oil to calm you, or lime or lemon to invigorate (add eight drops to a warm bath)

● A big luxurious towel, just for you

● Several candles to go around the tub

● A patterned shower curtain that lifts your spirits and your inner energy

● A bath loofah for body brushing

● A spider plant or fern to increase the room's energy

If you choose candles, always safely extinguish them after your bath.

STEP 49 YOUR WISH CARD

Before the end of your clearout, get one of your photocopied wish cards (see page 96) and write down your wish for your sublime bathroom, or choose one of the following.

"I want to make my bathroom a sensuous retreat."

"I long for a bathroom that honors my soul."

"I'd love a bathroom that fills me with tranquility."

"I want a bathroom full of inspiring scents."

"I am designing a bathroom that is my perfect retreat."

"I see my bathroom as my safe cocoon."

REAL-LIFE LETTING GO

A friend, Jane, always brought back some special shells from vacation for her bathroom collection. Although she always removed some before adding the new ones, she still spent more time cleaning the shells than her bathroom. When she asked for my help, I suggested she frame a collage of her favorite shells and discard the rest – a perfect solution to her dilemma.

The Attic Challenge

FOR A ROOM OF THE PAST: 8 HOURS

Step 50 – Complete the questionnaire (see pages 68–69) and rate your attic

Step 51 – Minimize your painting materials

Step 52 – Let go of school memorabilia

Step 53 – Part with love mementoes

Step 54 – Sort through your Christmas decorations

Step 55 – Rationalize your vacation box

Steps 56 & 57 – Your affirmation for success

STEP 50 MAKING A ROOM FOR LETTING GO

Take a deep breath and go up into your attic. Can you easily get through the door, or is it jammed with boxes of junk? (Check your answers to the questionnaire.)

● Are there bursting bags of old festive decorations and dusty boxes of old love trinkets lying around?

● Do you trip over boxes from your school days?

● Are shelves where you store your vacation and decorating materials in complete disorder?

The attic is a wonderful place to store any possessions that are rarely used. But if it is so full of junk that you don't dare go in there, you are making it into a black hole full of slow, sticky energy that literally hangs over the household. Try and think why you feel you need to keep such an attachment to your past. Write down how you see this place with the clutter removed.

STEP 51 PAINTING MATERIALS

Check for:

✓ Dried-up paint and varnish tins

✓ Stiff brushes of all sizes

✓ Rollers that were once spongy or fluffy

✓ Old cleaning liquids and paint-spattered rags

✓ Sample paint pots and stencils

✓ Broken paint trays

Most of us are proud of how we have decorated our homes, but you have no need to hang on to paint "souvenirs" from a color scheme that changed years ago. Paint changes color or dries up, and as our energy changes so does our taste in color. Your favorite shade of five years ago will be different today.

Get organized: Dump dried-up paint and cans of varnish; please contact your local sanitation department for regulations regarding disposal of hazardous waste. Keep any fresh cans to touch up walls after minor bumps and scrapes. Lose dried-up brushes and disposable rollers (keep the handles) broken items, rags, liquids, and stencils. Group paints in room order, place brushes neatly in jars for easy access.

Obvious benefits of clearout

You have an ordered decorating shelf or box.

Emotional benefits of clearout

You let go of those old decorating memories.

Maintenance: Review every time you decorate another room.

STEP 52 SCHOOL MEMORABILIA

Check for:

- ✔ Exercise or school books
- ✔ Badges, medals, sashes, scarves, and hats
- ✔ Awards, diplomas, and degrees
- ✔ College projects and essays
- ✔ School reports

Hanging on to boxes of material from your school and college days will just keep you entrenched in your childhood. Do you feel you have to justify what you have achieved, or were you happier in those days? You will always remember those times, but you are a different person now – so live in the present.

Get organized: Junk or recycle books, essays, and projects. Throw out long-forgotten awards; frame and display diplomas and degrees. Keep a small mementoes box with a few prize badges and other items for future generations.

Obvious benefits of clearout

A clean, empty corner in the attic.

Emotional benefits of clearout

Letting go of who you were, and celebrating who you are now.

Maintenance: This is a one-time clearout, but ask children to do a sort out before they leave home.

STEP 53 LOVE MEMENTOES

Check for:

- ✔ Yellowing love letters
- ✔ Pressed or dried flowers
- ✔ Photos of old boyfriends or girlfriends
- ✔ Love gifts, cards, old pieces of jewelry
- ✔ Books of love poems, cuddly toys

This is an emotive area to deal with as everyone remembers their first love or a special partner. But hoarding too much from your past relationships stops you from releasing these people or enjoying a current relationship to the full. It can also prevent you from meeting a new lover.

Get organized: Re-read love letters, keep some special ones, and trash the rest. Put a few cherished cards, photos, or letters in a special love treasures box in an accessible place for when you feel sentimental.

Obvious benefits of clearout

Extra attic space materializes.

Emotional benefits of clearout

You put your past relationships behind you.

Maintenance: Check every year, and after a relationship ends.

An attic is ideal storage, but don't overcrowd it and store labeled boxes neatly.

STEP 54 CHRISTMAS DECORATIONS

Check for:

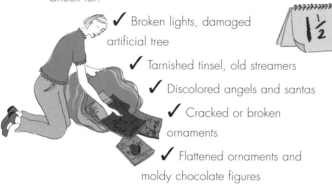

✔ Broken lights, damaged artificial tree

✔ Tarnished tinsel, old streamers

✔ Discolored angels and santas

✔ Cracked or broken ornaments

✔ Flattened ornaments and moldy chocolate figures

With each Christmas, more decorations seem to get added to the groaning box in the attic, but how many old ones are hung up? This is a sentimental time, but don't preserve ancient decorations for the sake of it; it prevents you from bringing in new ones and fresh seasonal energy.

Get organized: Dig into the box. Keep that favorite angel, but discard broken or tatty decorations. Check lights, and ditch defective ones; replace bulbs on working strings. Add a section divider, placing rolled-up tinsel and streamers in one, ornaments in another, and so on.

Obvious benefits of clearout

Usable decorations in a re-planned box.

Emotional benefits of clearout

You let go of Christmas pasts.

Maintenance: Check yearly in early December.

STEP 55 VACATION BOX

Check for:

✔ Last year's sun lotions and creams

✔ Broken or perished snorkels, masks, and fins

✔ Out-of-date insect repellent, half-empty first-aid kit

✔ Faded caps, torn sarongs, worn-out beach bags, unused travel games

✔ Travel hairdryer and plugs that don't work

After a vacation, don't throw your regular vacation gear back in its box – make sure it's worth keeping. Hoarding too much vacation junk can deplete the enjoyment of your next trip, so evaluate it before you go.

Get organized: Discard sunscreen lotions more than a year old – their protective properties are lost. Throw out worn-out travel goods; mend or junk broken items; give away games to other travelers; check the dates of first-aid kit contents; replace missing medicines.

Obvious benefits of clearout

You find what you want with ease.

Emotional benefits of clearout

You plan your next trip with a light heart.

Maintenance: Assess twice a year and see what useless goods have crept in.

SUMMARY

Well done – it is hard work to declutter here, but see how space is now emerging in this once overcrowded room.

Re-planned Store Room

STEP 56 ATTIC TREATS

Check for:

✓ Streamlining your decorating materials

✓ Letting go of your school memories

✓ Dealing with those love tokens

✓ Bringing some order to your vacation goods

✓ Saying goodbye to Christmas rejects

If you have had a bit of a struggle but still managed to do at least two of the above. you can allow yourself some treats to make your attic a more appealing space. Choose your own useful items, or select from the list below.

Clearout treats

● Easy-to-fix shelving

● A bulkhead light fitting to bring some light energy into this dingy room

● Hardwearing crates on wheels so that you can move them around

● Attractive labels so that you can find everything you store

● Inexpensive units with small drawers for those small accessories you need to keep

STEP 57 YOUR WISH CARD

Before you finish clearing out, take one of your photocopies of the card on page 96. Write down your own wish for your ideal attic, or choose one of the following:

"I aim to have an attic that has plenty of good storage."

"I'd like my attic to be full of ordered boxes and neat shelving."

"I want an attic that is a pleasure to go in."

"I desire an attic space with very little stored in it."

"I long for an attic with very few possessions from my past."

"I need an attic with easy access."

REAL-LIFE LETTING GO

A client, Chris, needed a lot of encouragement to junk the twenty years' worth of credit card statements stored in his attic. Although he realized that they were irrelevant to his life today and tied him to his younger self, long gone, he was using them to remember happy events from years gone by. When he saw how his nostalgia had really been overshadowing his present life, he found it easier to let go of those slips of paper.

The Home Office Challenge

FOR A ROOM OF CREATIVITY: 10½ HOURS

Step 58 – Complete the questionnaire (see pages 80–81 and study the home office

Step 59 – Inspect office equipment

Step 60 – Rake through filing cabinets (personal)

Step 61 – Check out filing cabinets (financial)

Step 62 – Look at the pinboard

Step 63 – Sort out desk correspondence

Step 64 – Appraise personal organizer/Palm pilot

Step 65 – Delete emails/unwanted computer files

Steps 66 & 67 – Your affirmation for success

STEP 58 MAKING A ROOM OF INSPIRATION

Have a look inside your office – the place where you spend all your days if you are self-employed. Does it fill you with dread every time you enter, because of the mess and unfinished tasks that exist there.

● Have you got equipment lying around that doesn't work?

● Are your filing cabinets and stationery units full of things you don't need?

● Do you have contact names, addresses, and correspondence that date back a long time?

● Is your computer clogged up with old emails, programs, and files?

A home office is where you handle the home's finances and correspondence, push forward new projects, and create future proposals. If there is clutter scattered all around you, you will work in a confused, disjointed way and not achieve the tasks you set yourself. Write down how you see your model working office.

STEP 59 OFFICE MACHINERY

Check for:

✓ Malfunctioning printers, photocopiers, and fax machines

✓ Old computers, or ones that keep crashing

✓ Crackly or noisy phones, faulty pocket recorders

If you are surrounded by machinery that is broken or not working properly in your office, it affects the vibrancy of the room's energy and can disrupt your communication with your clients. It also shows a lack of concern for how you run your business.

Get organized: Call in professionals to fix machines that are not working well; dispose of those that are broken, old, or used. Get faults fixed on phones, or replace if unrepairable.

Obvious benefits of clearout
A better functioning office with higher energy levels.
Emotional benefits of clearout
A feeling of satisfaction that you communicate properly with the outside world.

Maintenance: Have all major equipment serviced yearly; get problems fixed as soon as they occur.

STEP 60 FILING CABINETS (PERSONAL)

Check for:

✓ Papers from failed courses

✓ Divorce papers from years ago

✓ Hospital letters concerning past illnesses

✓ Clippings files of things you plan to do

✓ Vacation bookings dating back years

✓ Old society memberships

Personal files can easily fill up with excessive paperwork that soon dates, so they need to be patrolled regularly. Also if you are holding on to files that dealt with former break-ups, illnesses, or things not completed or done, you are linking into unnecessary negativity from your past.

Get organized: Keep current legal papers, bin old hospital and vacation correspondence, dated course material, and lapsed membership details. Label files clearly; ditch clippings more than a year old; retain those that are still useful; put current ones in plastic sleeves in a ring binder file.

Obvious benefits of clearout

Order is restored to your bulging cabinet.

Emotional benefits of clearout

You have a positive energy surge as old papers are released.

Maintenance: Have a major clearout yearly; do a quick check every three months.

Make sure that your desk area is neat and tidy so that you work in a postive way.

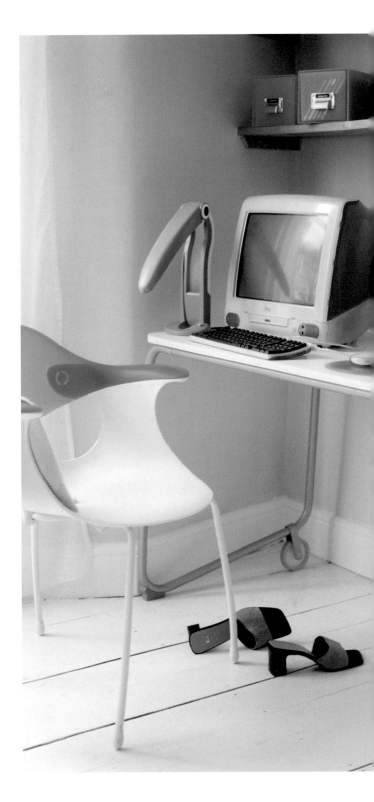

STEP 61 FILING CABINETS (FINANCIAL)

Check for:

✓ Papers relating to out of date loans

✓ Out-of-date insurances, accountant's correspondence, savings plans

✓ Mortgage papers from past properties

✓ Old letters to bank or pension companies, overdrawn bank statements, and credit card bills

Your office needs a vibrant atmosphere to deal with your home affairs or work successfully on business projects. If your financial filing cabinet is cluttered up with papers that relate to borrowings, defunct savings, or loans from years back, you are not encouraging a healthy flow of monies into your bank account.

Get organized: Throw away paperwork for paid-up loans and closed savings accounts. Retain important financial correspondence relating to the last few years; get rid of anything unimportant. If you are self-employed, keep the required bank statements for the necessary years, discard the remainder plus irrelevant credit card statements.

Obvious benefits of clearout
You find all your financial papers quickly.

Emotional benefits of clearout
The bond with old financial worries is broken.

Maintenance: Be strict with what you retain; purge files every six months and after financial changes.

STEP 62 PINBOARD

Check for:

✓ Notes more than six months old

✓ Old change-of-address cards, unused business cards

✓ Scribbled phone numbers, outdated contacts, and restaurant cards, old take-out menus

✓ Yellowing timetable for health club classes, last year's calendar

Pinboards are great places to store contact numbers for the people or places whom you regularly call. But if the board is clogged up with numerous old pieces of paper and unknown cards, you are creating an area of confusion and frustration where you never find what you want.

Get organized: Remove everything from the board methodically. Sort into useful and out-of-date piles, and discard the latter. Pin current cards and menus back on the board; transfer scrawled phone numbers to your organizer. Add this year's calendar and your latest gym timetable.

Obvious benefits of clearout
You can find the contact number you want.

Emotional benefits of clearout
A clearer head as another area of confusion disappears.

Maintenance: Every two months, remove any debris that has accumulated on the board.

STEP 63 DESK CORRESPONDENCE

Check for:

✔ Piles of letters over a week old

✔ Unpaid bills and invoices

✔ Unanswered invitations

✔ Piles of marketing and press information

✔ Unread reports, contracts

Your desk is the linchpin of your office. It is from here that you plan projects, give birth to new ideas, and run your day-to-day affairs. Submerging it in a mound of unanswered paperwork will make you feel disorientated and you'll work in a haphazard, distracted way.

Get organized: Be strict with yourself. Reply to letters and invitations the same day or email a reply, then file; have an invoice folder and set a weekly/monthly date to pay invoices; read promotional material, file anything useful, or throw out. Read reports and contracts, then pass them on or keep for reference.

Obvious benefits of clearout

You have desk space to work on tasks in hand.

Emotional benefits of clearout

Your mind clears and your concentration improves.

Maintenance: Work on having an empty desk each night; check weekly if the paper mountain starts to grow again.

STEP 64 PERSONAL ORGANIZERS

Check for:

- ✓ Contact details for people you no longer see
- ✓ Scraps of paper with phone numbers
- ✓ Post-its stuck on organizer
- ✓ Travel tickets, old notes, crumpled business cards, or shopping lists stuck inside

An organizer should live up to its name and help, rather than hinder, your daily working life. It is your ready access to your business and personal contacts, and needs to be full of positive people who will aid your working life. If it is bulging with trivia, or packed with old associates or disliked people, you are affecting your chances of business success.

Get organized: Remove extraneous pieces of paper and tickets, transfer useful information or numbers from notes and Post-its; carefully flick through crossing out unwanted details; re-write altered pages. Do the same with a Palm pilot, electronically deleting what is not needed.

Obvious benefits of clearout

An organizer that you can easily open where you can find the number you need.

Emotional benefits of clearout

You feel back in control, and can take on the world.

Maintenance: Review every six months. As contacts change, delete them. Check for accumulating junk every month.

STEP 65 EMAILS AND COMPUTER FILES

Check for:

- ✓ Unanswered emails
- ✓ Fifty-plus emails still in inbox
- ✓ Old project or correspondence files
- ✓ Unused programs

A computer is a valuable working tool, and like other equipment in your office, can have information overload. Seventy per cent of a computer's hard disk should be kept free for it to work fast and efficiently. So if you don't archive material regularly you, like your computer, will work more slowly and not progress with important projects or new ideas.

Get organized: Answer emails daily then delete, print out, or file in folders on your hard disk. Delete older, irrelevant files or archive onto back-up disks. Remove unused programs, or get professional help.

Obvious benefits of clearout

An efficient computer that is less prone to "crashing" or "freezing."

Emotional benefits of clearout

You feel a surge of creativity, and notice that you are achieving much more than usual.

Maintenance: Stay on top of your emails; regularly clear out files every three months. Have a professional overhaul on your computer every year.

SUMMARY

Well done – the atmosphere is now much more conducive to successful working.

Inspiring domain

STEP 66

Check for:

✓ Working office equipment

✓ Attacking all mail

✓ Pruning material in filing cabinets

✓ Renewing your pinboard

✓ De-junking old contacts

✓ Spring-cleaning your computer

An office is one of the worst areas for clutter, so don't be surprised if it is taking time to clear. If you have managed at least three – ideally four – of the above goals, you can get some treats to make your office a better place. Buy from the list below, or invent your own.

Clearout treats

● A peace lily or golden pothos plant to soak up computer emissions

● Transparent disk box, or stacking plastic boxes for stationery items

● An ergonomic, high-backed office chair for back support

● Packs of colored files

● A modern desk lamp to light your way

● A fan to keep the office cool through the summer

STEP 67 YOUR WISH CARD

Near the end of your clearout, choose a photocopy of the card on page 96. Write down your wish for your perfect office, or select from the following.

"I want an office that enhances my creativity."

"My dream office promotes my success."

"I desire a practical office space."

"I yearn for an office full of inspirational energy."

"I crave an office that helps me achieve my goals."

"I need an office that encourages my financial security."

REAL-LIFE LETTING GO

I could hardly enter Barbara's home office. Household items were beating a path out of the closets and office paperwork was piled up everywhere – from the floor to the edges of her desk, where she could barely locate the phone. Together we removed a lot of useless clutter, and she did more on her own. A few weeks later she rang me to say how different she felt – she had more energy, and had acquired three new clients.

The Front Garden Challenge

FOR AN AREA OF GROWTH: 13½ HOURS

Step 68 – Complete the questionnaire (see pages 84–85) and look around your front space

Step 69 – Appraise any damage to your fences or walls

Step 70 – Examine the condition of your gate

Step 71 – Deal with any builder's rubble

Step 72 – Look at the position of the trash cans

Step 73 – Trim overgrown shrubs

Step 74 – Study your path

Step 75– Check for rotting flowerpots

Step 76 – Hunt for any garden pests

Steps 77 & 78 – Your affirmation for success

STEP 68 MAKING A DESIRABLE SPACE

Stand outside your home and look toward your front space from the path. Do you really feel drawn to enter? Or do you feel upset because the whole area is so untidy and overgrown? (Check your answers to the questionnaire.)

● Are there overflowing trash cans and broken pots everywhere?

● Have your boundaries and path become run down or do they need a good de-junking?

● Do you fight with shrubs or creepy-crawlies to get to your front door?

If you are finding your front area unappealing, or have to battle to your front door, muse about how visitors must feel. The front of your home is the first impression that you give to people, so it needs to be attractive and appealing. If it is an utter mess, are you trying to stop people coming in? Put down on paper how you would like to change this space.

Maintenance: Clean out moss and weeds monthly. See if any renovation is necessary in the fall.

STEP 69 DAMAGED FENCES AND WALLS

Check for:

✓ Fence falling down or broken sections

✓ Frost-damaged, cracked, peeling, or broken wall

A wall or fence protects your property, giving you a safe boundary. But if it is in disrepair or falling down, ask yourself why you are subliminally removing boundaries with your neighbors and letting them intrude upon your personal space.

Get organized: Restore missing fence panels or sections, and paint or stain. Replace broken bricks or stones, and fill cracks, or have your wall rebuilt.

Obvious benefits of clearout
Your territory is now clearly demarcated.
Emotional benefits of clearout
Your personal boundaries are back inplace, you feel secure once more.

Maintenance: Search for any signs of decay every six months.

STEP 70 DILAPIDATED GATE

Check for:

✔ A gate falling off its hinges

✔ Peeling or rusting paintwork, rotting wood on gate and posts

✔ Weeds creeping up the posts and hinges

✔ Creaking, rusty hinges

A gate is the first way in to your home, so if it is neglected or falling apart, what impression do you think people have of your home and the way you live? It is as though you are trying to bar entrance to your sanctuary , so get it fixed and let visitors flow in once more.

Get organized: Repair the existing gate and posts or buy new ones, if they are wooden and rooted. Rub down old paintwork with glasspaper, and re-paint or varnish for protection.

Obvious benefits of clearout
A smart gate that operates smoothly.

Emotional benefits of clearout
A feeling of opening yourself up to new opportunities.

Maintenance: Check your gate each spring to see if anything needs oiling or renewing.

STEP 71 BUILDERS' RUBBLE

Check for:

✔ Old bags of sand, cement, bricks

✔ Removed fittings such as baths and toilets

✔ Pieces of wood, plasterboard, old carpet, or flooring

Make your front gate and path as appealing as possible to draw people in.

If your home is being renovated, inevitably there will be materials stored outside temporarily. But if the work is finished, and messy rubble piles are left behind, it is making a dead energy space that needs removing before family life is affected.

Get organized: The rubble is the builders' responsibility, so ask them to come back and remove it. Alternatively, take what you can to the dump, or pay someone to remove it.

Obvious benefits of clearout
You have reclaimed your space.

Emotional benefits of clearout
You are not annoyed approaching your home.

Maintenance: Make sure that builders remove any debris before they finish improvement works.

STEP 72 TRASH CANS

Check for:

✓ Trash can positioned near the front door or outside the home

✓ Decaying matter scattered around trash can

✓ Too much in bins

A trash can full of dirty containers and decaying matter is a major area of negative energy outside your home, so it should be positioned as far away from your front door as possible. If it is too close, it will blight the vibrancy of the chi that enters your home through the front door.

Get organized: Never place your trash can in direct line with your front door – always put it to one side. Clean up stray waste, bag up well to prevent odors escaping; try to keep it well away from scavenging animals.

Obvious benefits of clearout

You don't trip over the bin as you head toward your door.

Emotional benefits of clearout

You notice a better atmosphere in your hall.

Maintenance: Be vigilant about clearing up stray trash around the bin. If you get too many bags days before it is going to be collected, take them to the dump or waste center yourself.

STEP 73 OVERGROWN SHRUBS AND TREES

Check for:

✓ Trees overhanging path, taking over house

✓ Tall bush at front blocking light

✓ Overgrown creeper around door

✓ Prickly bushes or parasitical weeds by path

Overgrown shrubbery in your front area can make it gloomy and dark. If people are also pushing past branches or prickly bushes just to get to your door, many won't bother.

Get organized: Hack back overgrown shrubbery, prickly bushes, and strangling weeds, or get professional help to lighten the area and expose the pathway.

Obvious benefits of clearout

A front space that people want to enter.

Emotional benefits of clearout

A feeling of being opened up to the world again.

Maintenance: Do major work here each season; trim regularly each month.

STEP 74 UNKEMPT PATH

Check for:

✓ Broken or uneven paving stones or slabs

✓ Tall weeds or moss

✓ Overgrown plants

A path is a conduit for positive chi to enter your home. If you let it become overgrown with weeds or plants, or fall into general disrepair, you are disrupting this energy path and creating an unsettled, changeable atmosphere.

Get organized: Replace damaged stones or slabs; remove weeds or moss, and generally clean; cut back overgrown plants. Chi should move in spirals to the door, so try to lay a path in this pattern or add some pots or plants at different intervals to break up the straight energy flow.

Obvious benefits of clearout

You don't have to watch where to walk.

Emotional benefits of clearout

A more positive attitude as you approach your home.

Maintenance: Clean out moss and weeds monthly. See if any renovation is necessary in the fall.

Regularly dead-head flowers, cut back shrubs and cut the grass for an ordered garden.

STEP 75 ROTTING FLOWERPOTS

Check for:

✔ Pots with frost damage

✔ Cracks, chips, or moss on pots

✔ Dead plants, old compost in pots

Pots full of scented flowers around your front door or lining an apartment balcony draw admiring looks from all, and they make an area of positive energy and growth. But pots that are full of weeds or dead plants have an air of neglect, introducing a negative energy flow that affects everyone.

Get organized: Throw out pots beyond repair; clean up mossy ones and buy some new terra-cotta ones. Add new compost and healthy, seasonal flowering plants. Place one on each side of front door to attract in visitors.

Obvious benefits of clearout

A tidier, more appealing space.

Emotional benefits of clearout

You heart lifts looking at beautiful, healthy flowers.

Maintenance: Check the condition of pots every season; replace plants, renew compost.

STEP 76 GARDEN PESTS

Check for:

✔ Flies or other pests

✔ Slugs, snails, ants, and caterpillars

If you walk through your garden and everywhere you look you see pests eating away at your flowers and vegetables, you have a big problem to resolve. Apart from the bad effect on all your plants, if the pests are in control, symbolically you are allowing all the goodness to be sucked out of your life.

Get organized: Try to use organic methods to get bugs under control as insecticides will pollute the environment. Remove slugs and snails with animal-friendly pellets; cut back badly nibbled plants.

Physical benefits of clearout

Healthier-looking plants and vegetables.

Emotional benefits of clearout

More energy and a feeling of balance as your plants get back to normal.

Maintenance: Examine every week in the spring and summer months.

SUMMARY

Don't be disheartened if you haven't managed everything. You have made a good start and your front space is starting to have an appealing atmosphere.

Glorious flowering pots add vibrancy and structure to your balcony or yard.

Inspiring space

STEP 77 FRONT YARD/GARDEN REWARDS

Check for:

✓ Sorting out your flowerpots

✓ Hacking back overgrown shrubbery

✓ Repairing gates and fences

✓ Renewing the path to your door

✓ Clearing away builders' rubbish

✓ Tidying up your trash cans

✓ Getting rid of excessive bugs

Are you exhausted? Clearing out the garden can be hard work, but if you have gotten through at least four, hopefully five, of the above goals, your front area is well on its way to being approachable once more, and you deserve a few treats. Choose from the list below, or invent your own.

Clearout treats:

● A bird table

● A five-rod wind chime for the front door to slow down incoming chi

● Big terra-cotta or ceramic pots for welcoming flowers for your entrance

● Hanging baskets

● Small water fountain (on left-hand side as you look out of your front door) to boost chi flow

● Trellis fencing to grow scented climbers

STEP 78 YOUR WISH CARD

Toward the end of your clearout, pick one of your photocopies of the card on page 96. Note down your wish for your special front space from the following, or think of one of your own.

"I want a front area that people are drawn to."

"I dream of a front space with alluring scents."

"I yearn for the front of my home to have structure and order."

"I seek a front space with a charming ambience."

"I desire a front area that I long to go home to."

"My perfect front space is full of flowering shrubs."

REAL-LIFE LETTING GO

Roger had become reclusive after his previous relationship ended. As I fought my way past all the shrubs to his front door, I realized how he was subconsciously pushing people away. I told him that he needed to clear this area and make it more inviting. He followed my advice and, about a month later, he called to say that his social life was improving and he had invited a woman to dinner that night.

The Back Garden Challenge

FOR A VERDANT RETREAT: 13½ HOURS

Step 79 – Complete the questionnaire (see page 84–85) and pace around your backyard or garden

Step 80 – Check for any blocked drains

Step 81 – Search for dying flowers

Step 82 – Delve in the pond

Step 83 – Sort out any dead tree stumps

Step 84 – Work on the overcrowded shed

Step 85 – Renovate garden furniture

Step 86 – Look at any garden statues

Steps 87 & 88 – Your affirmation for success

STEP 79 MAKING A SPECIAL RETREAT

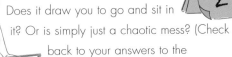

Stand at your back door and note your impressions of your back space. Does it draw you to go and sit in it? Or is simply just a chaotic mess? (Check back to your answers to the questionnaire.)

● Are you accosted by the unpleasant odor of blocked drains, a stagnant pond, and a dying tree?

● Can you never find your faded garden furniture in your overcrowded shed?

● Do you keep meaning to cut back old flowers and update any statues you own?

The backyard or back garden is your place for growing plants, relaxation, and entertaining. If you are surrounded by junk and decaying items, the atmosphere will reflect this and you will not want to linger here. Write down the ways in which you can transform this space.

STEP 80 BLOCKED DRAINS

Check for:

✓ Overflowing drain

✓ Leaves, twigs, garden debris

✓ Unpleasant smell

Keeping everything working efficiently in your home and backyard is important, because any problems create an energy block that can slow down the functioning of your household. Blocked drains prevent the natural water draining process, producing stale, bad-smelling water, so they need to be sorted out straight away.

Get organized: Clear out all the debris in the drain and add some cleansing fluid. If it is still not working well, call out some professionals.

Obvious benefits of clearout

The blockage is removed and water flows away freely once more.

Emotional benefits of clearout

As the chi movement improves, so does your family interaction.

Maintenance: Keep a vigilant eye on drains. If you notice any flooding out back, check immediately. Clean out regularly, particularly in the fall when there are a lot of leaves around.

STEP 81 DYING FLOWERS

Check for:

✓ Plants attacked by bugs, fungal, or viral disease

✓ Flowers past their best

Like your home, your yard or garden needs to be a vibrant area, full of healthy, growing plants, particularly the flowering varieties. If you look out of your back door and see a mass of wilted or dying flowers, doesn't the low energy there make you feel depressed? Keep your garden looking good and your inner chi stays high.

Get organized: Dead-head any old flowers to allow for new flowering; cut back any plants under attack from bugs. Replace dead plants with seasonal flowering varieties.

Obvious benefits of clearout

A tidy backyard or garden full of healthy plants.

Emotional benefits of clearout

Your spirits rise looking at the glorious flowers you have planted.

Maintenance: Regularly dead-head during the summer; review plants each spring and fall.

Look after all your garden furniture, so that you can set it out each year for summer dining on your patio.

STEP 82 THE POND

Check for:

✓ Stagnant, murky water, floating leaves

✓ Sick fish

✓ Dying plants, slimy residue

A pond can be a vital part of a garden, especially if it contains fish, as they help to keep the water moving, encouraging the general circulation of positive energy. But if has been neglected, it becomes a liability as the stagnant water can have a detrimental effect on the family's finances.

Get organized: Remove stagnant water and clean out the pond, getting rid of dead plants and sick fish. Fill with clean water and install a small pump to keep the water flowing and encourage good chi. Add a filter to keep the water fresh; restock with rocks, plants, water lilies, and fish – in feng shui, nine fish are considered auspicious.

Obvious benefits of clearout

A clean, vibrant pond that is a joy to look at.

Emotional benefits of clearout

A black cloud lifts from you as you eliminate the negativity that existed here.

Maintenance: Do minor cleaning tasks weekly. Check filter and pump following manufacturer's instructions. Have a major clearout once a year.

STEP 83 DEAD TREE STUMPS

Check for:

✓ Rotting stump from felled tree

✓ Dying tree

An old tree stump is one of the worst things to have in your back space. It emits negative, dead energy, which floods out into the rest of the garden; ultimately it may affect the healthy atmosphere of your home.

Get organized: Have the stump dug out completely as soon as possible. Or, place a large chunk of clear quartz on it to counteract the decay. Call in a tree surgeon for advice on dying or unhealthy trees.

Obvious benefits of clearout

This dying eyesore is removed from sight.

Emotional benefits of clearout

The lethargy that has become part of your life finally lifts.

Maintenance: Check your trees each season. At any sign of decay, seek professional advice.

STEP 84 OVERCROWDED SHED OR OUTBUILDING

Check for:

✓ Rusting garden tools, perished hoses, watering cans, paddling pools

✓ Broken garden chairs, tables, or umbrellas

✓ Old fertilizer, plant liquids, seeds, pots

✓ Decrepid bicycles, sports equipment

✓ Useless gadgets and junk, broken barbecue set and mower.

If you can't get the door open to your shed, it has probably become your next junking ground as your attic is full. Don't think that just because it is outside it won't affect you – your shed is still draining your home's overall energy. A shed is a good storage area for garden accessories and outdoor equipment in regular use, so make sure that this is what it contains.

Get organized: Trash any junk, old plant foods, and seeds, and equipment that is beyond repair. Put everything that you want to keep on the lawn or deck, then clean the shed well. Salvage and oil any rusty tools worth keeping. Get as much off the shed floor as possible by adding more shelves for items such as fertilizers and flower food; hang working tools and equipment on hooks or on peg rails. Keep any garden chairs and barbecue equipment stored by the door for easy access; padlock to keep kids out.

Obvious benefits of clearout

You now have a well-ordered storage space.

Emotional benefits of clearout

There is no longer a sense of dread as you enter your shed.

Maintenance: Clutter creeps back. Clear out seasonally – every three months.

Use the warm, soft light of candles to illuminate the way to your yard's dining space.

STEP 85 GARDEN FURNITURE

Check for:

✓ Peeling paint, faded wood color

✓ Ripped or stained cushions, torn fabric

✓ Broken or cracked struts or supports

Garden furniture is dragged out in the summer months to take advantage of entertaining on sunny days, and then it is often left to languish for the rest of the year. If you neglect it, allowing chairs and tables to fall into disrepair, you are affecting the feelings of support and comfort needed in your life.

Get organized: Check over furniture. Ditch any ancient pieces and replace; repair broken supports and replace fabric or cushions, if worthwhile. Rub down painted furniture with glasspaper and re-paint; re-stain colored woods.

Obvious benefits of clearout

Your furniture works properly and looks like new.

Emotional benefits of clearout

You no longer feel ashamed to bring out your garden furniture.

Maintenance: Clean well before storing each fall; check for repairs and any necessary replacements each spring.

STEP 86 GARDEN STATUES

Check for:

✓ Frightening gargoyles, demons, or imps

✓ Figures with broken arms or heads

✓ Overgrown or neglected statues

Your backyard or back garden should be a tranquil, relaxing place, so be careful what statuary you place there. Scary statues can generate a bad atmosphere, while broken male or female figures can symbolically encourage a health problem for a family member.

Get organized: Get rid of frightening or broken statues; scrub neglected ones. Display entwined or cupid statues to boost a relationship. Place a crane statue at the front and a tortoise at the back of the garden for harmony and a long life.

Obvious benefits of clearout

You garden looks less of a junk yard.

Emotional benefits of clearout

The balanced ambience means you feel calmer.

Maintenance: Clean well twice a year, and more frequently after inclement weather.

SUMMARY

Congratulate yourself; you have made a good start. Your backyard is really taking shape, so take some time out to sit there and admire it.

Glorious refuge

STEP 87 backyard/GARDEN REWARDS

Check for:

✓ Purging your pond

✓ Removing decaying tree stumps

✓ Tackling your heaving shed

✓ Revamping your garden furniture

✓ Cutting back any wilting flowers

✓ Clearing any blocked drains

Do you feel pleased with yourself? Even if you have not tackled all the garden tasks you wanted, if you have managed at least three of the above goals, you can allow yourself a few treats. Select from the list below, or invent your own.

Clearout treats

● A garden umbrella for shade and protection

● Garden lanterns or flares for summer entertaining

● A sun lounger to help you re-energize

● A hammock

● A barbecue or new accessories

● Strings of lights to illuminate the pathways

STEP 88 YOUR WISH CARD

As you finish your clearout, draw a card from your photocopies of the card on page 96. Write your wish for your idyllic back space from the following, or invent your own.

"I want my backyard (garden) to be an oasis of calm."

"I desire a backyard that is a magical haven."

"I see my back space as a Mediterranean paradise."

"I crave a backyard full of friends and laughter."

"I seek a back area where I can meditate and escape the world."

"My exquisite backyard has a hidden patio for romantic dining."

REAL-LIFE LETTING GO

Julie could not understand why her friends never seem to want to come around for barbecues. When I examined her backyard, I found a patio littered with weatherbeaten furniture surrounded by tubs full of weeds. On my advice, she purchased new furniture and an attractive umbrella, and filled her tubs with glorious summer blooms. The atmosphere changed completely, and soon her friends were flocking around to see her.

Clear your Emotions

TO CLEANSE YOUR HEAD

Step 89 – Complete the questionnaire (see pages 90–91) and assess problems that are holding you back

Step 90 – Analyze worries or problems

Step 91 – Think about self-criticism

Step 92 – Relax your mind

Step 93 – Let go of old lovers

Step 94 – Evaluate a relationship that has gone bad

Step 95 – Drop friends who drain your energy

Step 96 – Sort out irrational fears

Step 97 – Deal with inner anger

Step 98 – Release your own limitations

Step 99 – Get rid of imposed habits

Steps 100 & 101 – Your affirmation for success

STEP 89 WORKING OUT INNER TURMOIL

Fill in the questionnaire to find out where your problems lie. Some hurts may be rooted in your subconscious, so be patient with yourself as you work through these projects. You'll be surprised at what arises from your inner depths.

● Think about your life recently. Can you identify a constant annoyance?

● Is there something disturbing you long-term, which goes back to your childhood?

● Are you feeling overworked and stressed at the end of each day?

● Do you feel depressed, but don't really know what is wrong?

To get the most out of life, you need to be cleansed mentally and emotionally. Visualize how good you will feel when you have worked through your problem.

STEP 90 LETTING GO OF WORRIES

Check for:

✓ Worrying about problems daily

✓ Getting stressed about having an accident every time you travel

✓ Feeling nervous and unsettled about life continually

When you worry constantly, you create a fog of negativity around you. It wastes energy, cluttering up your mind so you can't think clearly. Keep fretting about a minor irritation, and your mind turns it into a major problem as all your attention is directed toward it. Worrying can become a miserable habit.

Healing vibrations: Clear your mind of all its clutter by doing a "clearing" meditation at the end of the day: focus on the good events that you want to happen, and think about the positives in your life.

Immediate benefits of clearout

A feeling of relief and a sense of calm that you have started to free yourself from worry.

Long-term benefits of clearout

You have a more confident approach to life, and look forward to the future.

Maintenance: Clear your mind of clutter every day to keep you worry-free.

STEP 91 ENDING SELF-CRITICISM

Check for:

✓ Always putting yourself down in public

✓ Criticizing your body image

✓ Never believing an attractive partner will like you

✓ Still needing approval from parents

If you are self-critical and feel unlovable, you have low self-esteem. This often stems from childhood where lack of praise or approval from your parents may have had you striving hard to get their love and attention.

Healing vibrations: Go for a day without criticizing yourself; clear out the past – visualize yourself as a child receiving praise from your parents; stand in front of a mirror daily and say: "I love you", buy new clothes and tell yourself how good you look in them.

Immediate benefits of clearout

Your self-confidence begins to return, and you feel happier getting up in the morning.

Long-term benefits of clearout

You realize you are a lovable person.

Maintenance: Tell yourself daily how great you are; pin a weekly affirmation on your bathroom mirror, and repeat twenty times a day.

STEP 92 CALMING YOUR MIND BEFORE BED

Check for:

✓ Waking up in the night remembering something you should have done at work

✓ Being unable to go to bed because your mind is still on overload

✓ Tossing and turning for an hour or so before sleep

✓ Only sleeping about five hours a night

Sleeping is the time when the body and mind can switch off, allowing you compete relaxation and rejuvenation. If your mind is still filled with the buzz of a busy day, it will disturb your normal sleep pattern so that you awake tired, irritable, and unrefreshed.

Healing vibrations: Sink into a bath with a few drops of lavender essential oil in the water, visualizing the day's aggravations drifting away; write down things to do before sleep; lose yourself in calming music.

Immediate benefits of clearout

You feel calm and tension-free before sleep.

Long-term benefits of clearout

You sleep better because your mind is relaxed.

Maintenance: Wind down daily before bed so that you always get your full quota of sleep.

STEP 93 RELEASING OLD LOVERS

Check for:

✓ Pictures of ex-partners everywhere

✓ Always comparing new partners with old

✓ Reminiscing about your past relationships

If you are surrounded by pictures of your ex-lovers, you constantly talk about them or keep remembering some experience that you shared, you are not breaking the bonds with them to allow a new, successful relationship to come in or to thrive. Yes, remember the good times, but those relationships are in the past and you need to live in, and enjoy the present.

Healing vibrations: Take down pictures of old partners and store just a few in your mementoes box (see page 39). To release a partner, visualize your ex-lover and see the bond between you as a cord which you then cut with scissors. Say to yourself, "I release you with love to enjoy your life with someone else".

Immediate benefits of clearout

You feel liberated as you let your past go.

Long-term benefits of clearout

You cut the link with old lovers and allow a new love to come in, or to grow.

Maintenance: Grieve when a relationship ends, but then do the meditation above and move on.

STEP 94 DEALING WITH A DETERIORATING RELATIONSHIP

Check for:

✓ Constantly arguing with partner

✓ Always feeling put down and criticized

✓ Not communicating well; lack of a sex life

For a relationship to thrive, there needs to be communication on all levels. If this has broken down, upsets can be caused by the smallest disagreements. If these are left to fester, the gulf can become wide. In turn, your energies are no longer in tune and that intimacy you once enjoyed can evaporate.

Healing vibrations: Discuss with your partner what is wrong, and what you can both do to resolve it. If there is a serious rift, suggest joint counselling to see if the relationship can be saved.

Immediate benefits of clearout

You feel better because your problems are out in the open and being discussed.

Long-term benefits of clearout

You are working on improving your relationship – only time will tell whether it can survive.

Maintenance: Talk through any issues when they first come up, don't let a deep rift develop.

STEP 95 LIMITING ENERGY VAMPIRES

Check for:

✓ Friends calling late to discuss their problems

✓ Dreading checking your answering machine

✓ Your friends mirroring something in you

It's easy to spot energy vampires. They are friends whose long phone calls drain you. And it is only afterwards that you realize that they haven't discussed your problems at all. But be careful – they could be mirroring a side of you. You may have been like that in the past, but are changing and no longer want one-sided, often negative, conversations.

Healing vibrations: Limit your phone time; if they call, be honest and say how you feel. If the friendship is over, explain your reasons and move on. As you grow, your energy changes; so will your friends.

Immediate benefits of clearout

You feel less depleted and your energy surges.

Long-term benefits of clearout

You see more of the people who nurture you.

Maintenance: Check your behavior if you're tempted to moan to your friends. Equally, beware of a new friend who calls you to discuss only their problems.

STEP 96 HALTING IRRATIONAL FEARS

Check for:

✔ Worries such as not locking your home before you leave, or it burning down when you're on vacation

✔ Constantly thinking that you will get seriously ill

✔ Convincing yourself that you'll have a road accident

Nowadays, most of us are aware that if we think positively about events, we make them happen. Yet this also works negatively: expect the worst, and eventually it happens. We all have the power to create our own reality – just make it a happy, joyful one.

Healing vibrations: Focus on the positives. Rather than worry about potential illness, say, "I am leading a happy, healthy life". Be confident when you step in a car and when you go away, think, "My home will be safe and secure while I'm on vacation".

Immediate benefit of clearout
You start to feel good about your life.

Long-term benefits of clearout
You slip occasionally, but you are gradually letting go of negative patterns.

Maintenance: If you start to worry about a future event, see yourself overcoming any glitches.

STEP 97 ABSOLVING ANGER

Check for:

✔ Suffering from mild depression and/or anxiety

✔ Always feeling guilty or resentful

✔ Irritability and always playing the martyr

We may not always feel proud of our anger, but it is a passionate energy: when it flows, it can make us more assertive. But if we suppress it, it festers, often turning into anxiety, irritability, and a feeling of struggle. It needs to be released or, in time, it can become one cause of drug dependency, or general ill health.

Healing vibrations: Express your anger. Try writing down the problem, or compose a letter to the person concerned to vent your grievances. But don't send it; burn it. Or take your annoyance out on a cushion, punching it and shouting out what is upsetting you. Deal with the emotion before attempting forgiveness. If you can cope, talk through your feelings with the person concerned. Don't be hurtful back as it only causes resentment and doesn't solve the problem.

Immediate benefits of clearout
You feel freer as you release all that pent-up anger.

Long-term benefits of clearout
Your inner resentment evaporates, and you are more open about your feelings.

Maintenance: Release your anger regularly as it arises to clear the air so you don't brood on issues.

STEP 98 BANISH SELF-LIMITATIONS

Check for:

✔ Not achieving what you want in life

✔ No belief in your self-worth

Many of us have some internal programming that stops us realizing our full potential. Often it is self-doubt – that inner voice that holds us back from being successful in our careers or relationships. You can change the program and turn your life around.

Healing vibrations: Work on removing your self-doubts. For example, for a new career, visualize a successful interview; then see yourself signing your contract and finally sitting in your new workspace. If you desire a new sports car, see it parked outside your door – see the color and model, then imagine yourself driving it and touching it. Sense how good the feeling is. Remember, as you visualize, really believe that your desire will come true.

Immediate benefits of clearout

You start noticing how easily you accomplish small objectives.

Long-term benefits of clearout

You are amazed at the goals you have now attained.

Maintenance: Banish the words "I can't" from your vocabulary – remember you can consciously set the pattern for how you want your life to be.

STEP 99 LETTING GO OF CHILDHOOD PATTERNS

Check for:

✔ Constantly repeating negative situations

✔ Displaying fixed attitudes

✔ Beliefs that are holding you back

Without us realizing it, our beliefs, both good and bad, are instilled in our subconscious from childhood. It is the bad beliefs, however, held by our "inner child" that ultimately hold us back from progressing in life. For example, if you were constantly fed negative beliefs such as "You will never be good looking", or "You will always have to work hard to earn money", these get stuck in your psyche; and you play them out in your adult life. You need to abandon these beliefs to change for the better.

Healing vibrations: Overcome negative beliefs by meditating to meet your inner child: visualize yourself at six years old in the home that you were living in then. As you talk with the child and become his or her friend, you will discover the beliefs that are holding you back now. Here's an example: Jess realized that subconsciously she always felt that her partners would leave her. When she visited her inner child, she found out that her father had favored her elder sister. This hurt and betrayal was being repeated in her adult life, as she always assumed that men would let her down. Whatever you inner child first tells you, repeat the visualization regularly to see your child and positively replay any interaction that has caused you hurt. To heal her negative beliefs, Jess revisited her inner child and recreated situations where she was the focus of her father's love – his little princess – to reverse this adult pattern.

Immediate benefits of clearout

Relief at finding out why you are repeating certain patterns.

Long-term benefits of clearout

A wonderful feeling of release as you start to reverse negative beliefs.

Maintenance: Work regularly with this inner part of you to resolve deep-rooted problems.

SUMMARY

Be pleased with whatever you have managed to work through. You are on your way to being a better, more rounded person.

Spiritual release

STEP 100 EMOTIONAL DECLUTTERING REWARDS

Check for:

✓ Worrying less

✓ Letting go of past partners

✓ Being less self-critical

✓ Clearing out problems before sleep

✓ Confronting draining friends

✓ Showing your anger

✓ Banishing old fears

✓ Working on patterns from childhood

✓ Facing up to relationship problems

✓ Being aware of what is limiting you

If you have been working hard on improving yourself, and have started dealing with at least five of the above goals, you deserve some treats. Choose from the following list, or invent some of your own.

Clearout treats

● A self-development book to further your emotional progress

● A relaxation CD

● A body massage to release stress and tension

● A meditation class, to learn how to practice the technique effectively

● An appropriate space-clearing spray to clear your aura and your bedroom before sleep, or add some lavender essential oil to water in a mister bottle

● A flower remedy to help your current situation

STEP 101 YOUR WISH CARD

As you are working on your emotional self, take a photocopy of the wish card on page 96, and write down what you wish to transform. Choose from the following, or compose your own.

"I want to be a happy, joyful person."

"I deserve a loving, harmonious relationship."

"I have a circle of friends I adore."

"I am no longer limited by old beliefs."

"I am letting go of all my fears."

"I can accomplish anything I desire."

REAL-LIFE LETTING GO

James was always working long hours, and his family life was suffering. Tired with his over-achieving, he was persuaded by his wife to try a meditation to find out what was driving him. He discovered that his parents wanted to live out their dreams through him, so that nothing he ever did as a child was good enough. Through practicing meditation, he mentally re-ran childhood scenarios in which he had not always gotten the highest grade in his class or won a race, but this time he imagined feeling comfortable with *what* he had achieved. By regularly meditating, he started to let go of his workaholic tendencies.

Your Clutter Notebook

In this section of the book, you identify your personal clutter chaos by completing the questionnaires and sketching simple diagrams of your existing rooms.

First, fill in the questionnaires that are included on the Home, the Home Office, the Yard/Garden, and your Emotional Clutter, so that you can assess where you are overcrowded and where your junk is gathering, or what inner problems are holding you back from achieving your full potential. Next, study the sample diagrams for inside the home (see pages 70–79, 82–83) that indicate the likely places where piles of clutter gather and inhibit the positive flow of energy through your rooms. Now spend some time drawing in your own rooms on the graph pages provided, following the instructions with the diagrams, and see where your clutter hot spots are located. When you know where your problem areas exist, you can prioritize where to start clearing out, following the book's projects and adding in any that are specific to your home.

Drawing your plans

When you draw a plan of your hall or another room, it doesn't have to be to scale. Draw in the shape of the room and mark in the furniture and fittings you have there. Mark in bold with an "x" in red pen where clutter piles exist. Now draw in your first chi flow with a colored pen, starting at the door, indicating how it moves around the room in spirals until it exits by a window on the other side of the room. Then, using another colored pen, mark the chi energy coming back in the same window or one next to it, and show its flow around the room until it finally goes out through the door.

With the hall, show two chi flows coming through the door, one going up the stairs (if you have stairs) and the other continuing along the hall. You will now see clearly how your clutter piles are inhibiting the flow of energy around this area, and be able to identify where you need to take urgent action.

Is Your Clutter Taking Over?

Fill in this questionnaire to find out if clutter is taking over in your home.

YES   NO   SOMETIMES

1 Do you always feel overwhelmed by your clutter when you enter your home?
   If your answer is yes, write down below the major items that are cluttering your hall:

❶ _____   ❷ _____
❸ _____   ❹ _____
❺ _____   ❻ _____
❼ _____   ❽ _____
❾ _____   ❿ _____

2 Are you irritated by the disorder in your home but unable to make a start on it?

3 Are you always buying items that you don't really need but just fancy buying?

4 Is your home full of possessions you have inherited?

If your answer is yes, write down below what they are:

❶ _____   ❷ _____
❸ _____   ❹ _____
❺ _____   ❻ _____
❼ _____   ❽ _____
❾ _____   ❿ _____

5 Do you hang onto useless equipment or possessions because you feel they may be useful sometime?

6 Are you quite organized but living with someone who can't throw anything away?

7 Can you easily find your keys and mobile phone each morning?

8 Is your attic a dumping ground for things you don't use, or items from your past?

9 Do you buy the latest exercise equipment but soon lose interest and leave them to fester?

10 Are your kids copying your hoarding habit and refusing to give away any of their toys?

11 Have you brought boxes from your old home that you still haven't opened?

12 Are there files lurking somewhere that contain bank or credit card statements that are more than five years old?

13 Do you still have some of your goods stored in your parents' attic?

14 Is your bedroom an overcrowded room that depresses you?

If your answer is yes, list the areas where you have clutter:

❶ _____   ❷ _____
❸ _____   ❹ _____
❺ _____   ❻ _____
❼ _____   ❽ _____
❾ _____   ❿ _____

15 Do you regularly throw out or give away the clothes you don't wear?

16 Is your bathroom really overcrowded with beauty and cleaning products?

17 Are you determined to get rid of all your junk, but feel frightened of losing its protection?

18 Are you depressed and lethargic because your home is such a mess?

	YES	NO	SOMETIMES

19 Close your eyes and visualize how you would feel if one of your cluttered areas was cleared. Do you get a feeling of relief and satisfaction?

20 Now close your eyes and visualize your home as clean and ordered with good storage units. Does this make you feel more in control?

21 Do you have problems letting go of sentimental possessions?

If your answer is yes, list the type of possessions you have kept:

❶ _____ ❷ _____
❸ _____ ❹ _____
❺ _____ ❻ _____
❼ _____ ❽ _____
❾ _____ ❿ _____

22 Do you have a clearout every six months to get rid of things you don't use?

23 Do you dispose of junk mail straight away, and open your mail daily to check statements or pay bills?

24 Is it normal for you to ask your family to clean up regularly?

25 Can you move around your living room easily?

If your answer is no, list what is taking up space in your living area:

❶ _____ ❷ _____
❸ _____ ❹ _____
❺ _____ ❻ _____
❼ _____ ❽ _____
❾ _____ ❿ _____

26 Are your videos and DVDs neatly stacked in a cupboard or rack?

27 Have you kept virtually every photograph you have taken?

28 Is it hard to see your kitchen worktops because there is so much equipment on them?

If your answer is yes, write down what you have on your worktops:

29 Do you let your bin overflow before you empty it?

30 Do you have lots of different cookery books that you never use?

TOTAL SCORE

Score two points for a "Yes", one for a "Sometimes", and zero for a "No."

40–60
Clutter seems to be taking over in your home and affecting your moods, depleting your energy levels and inhibiting your progress. Take a long look at the areas that are causing you problems and immediately schedule in time to start decluttering, following the steps in the seven projects on pages 10–41. This is your path to a junk-free life.

20–39
You are not yet sinking under masses of clutter, but it is starting to irritate you. If you don't sort it now, it will only get worse and affect your home life. Focus on the worst areas, following the seven projects on pages 10–41.

19 and under
Clutter is not yet a problem, but it can grow easily, so get to grips with it now – before it starts to control you. Search for suspect corners, then follow the steps in the seven projects on pages 10–41, and deal with the junked-up areas.

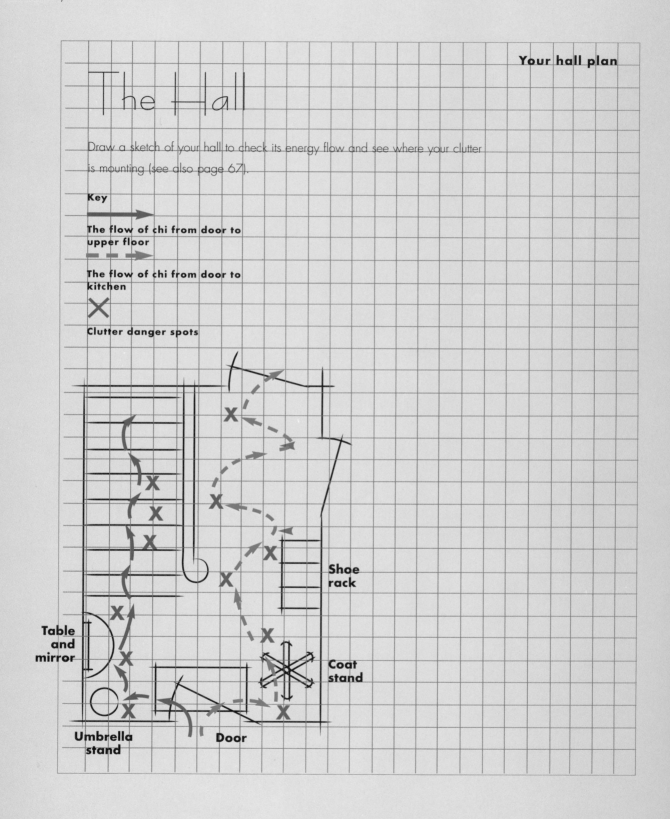

Your hall plan

The Hall

Draw a sketch of your hall to check its energy flow and see where your clutter is mounting (see also page 67).

Key

The flow of chi from door to upper floor

The flow of chi from door to kitchen

Clutter danger spots

Shoe rack

Table and mirror

Coat stand

Umbrella stand

Door

Your kitchen plan

The Kitchen

Draw a sketch of your kitchen, marking on its energy flow and to see where your clutter is mounting (see also pages 67 and 72).

The Living Room

Draw your living room following the example below, highlighting your clutter piles and chi flow (see also page 67).

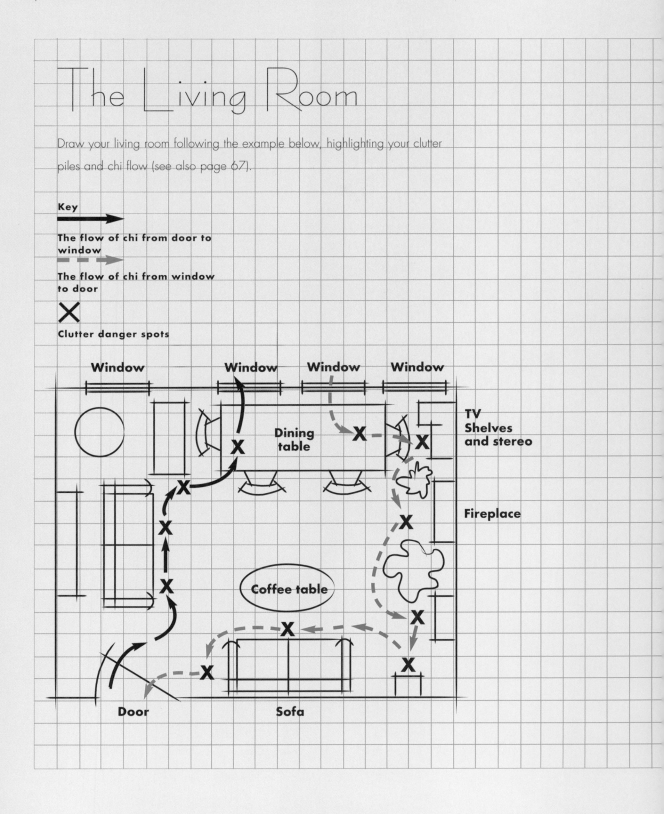

Key

The flow of chi from door to window

The flow of chi from window to door

X Clutter danger spots

Window   **Window**   **Window**   **Window**

Dining table

TV Shelves and stereo

Fireplace

Coffee table

Door   **Sofa**

Your living room plan

The Bedroom

Draw in your bedroom in the same style as the example below, and mark in your clutter piles and chi flow (see also pages 67 and 72).

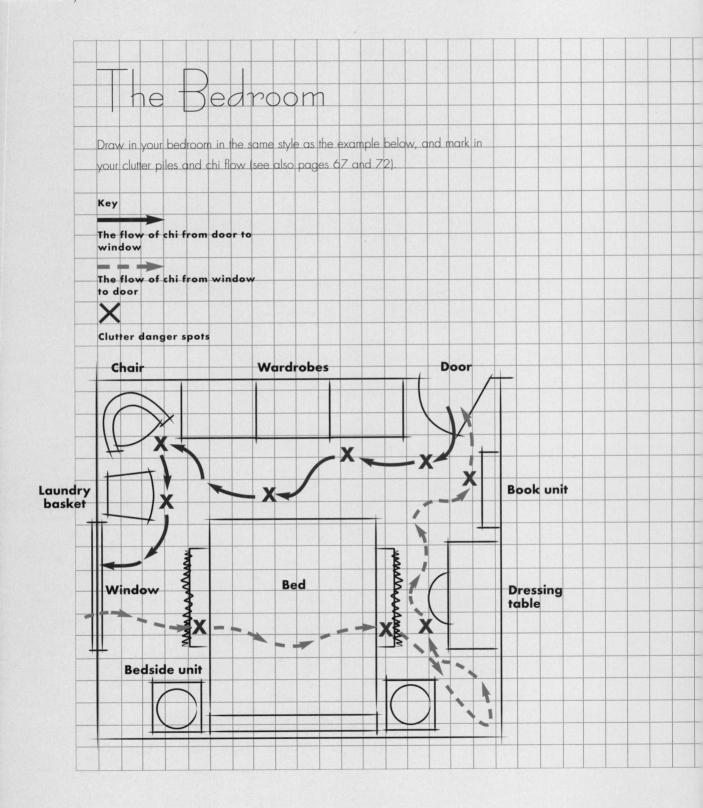

Key

The flow of chi from door to window

The flow of chi from window to door

✗

Clutter danger spots

Your bedroom plan

The Child's Bedroom

Draw in your child's and guest bedrooms to see the energy flow and find out where the clutter lurks (see pages 67 and 72).

Key

———▶

The flow of chi from door to window

– – –▶

The flow of chi from window to door

✗

Clutter danger spots

Your child's bedroom plan

The Bathroom

Draw in your bathroom plan as shown below, and highlight your clutter piles and the flow of chi (see also pages 67 and 72).

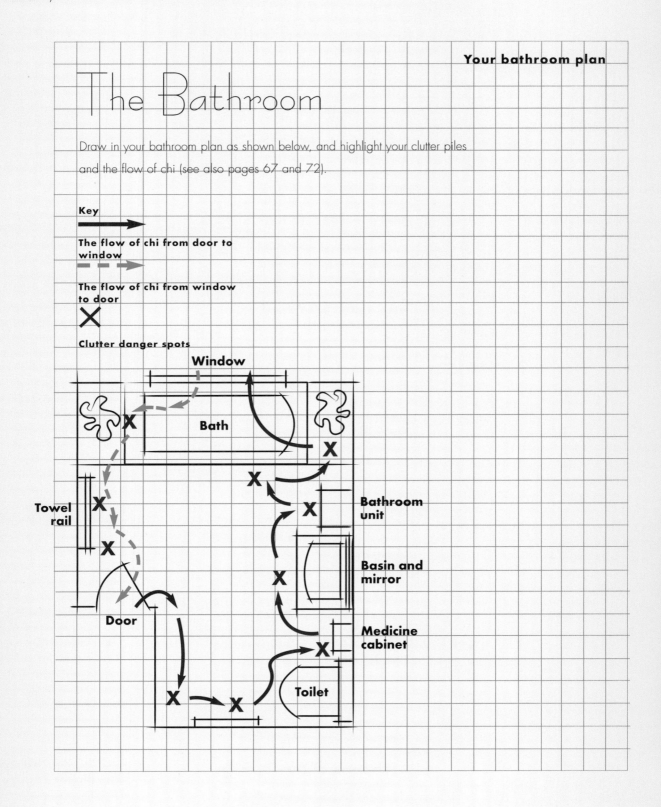

Key

The flow of chi from door to window

The flow of chi from window to door

X

Clutter danger spots

Window

Bath

Towel rail

Bathroom unit

Basin and mirror

Medicine cabinet

Door

Toilet

Your attic plan

The Attic Plan

Draw a plan of your attic to see what clutter piles are stopping the energy flow. Indicate only one flow of chi – show it coming through the door and circulating clockwise around the obstacles in the room and out of the door again (see pages 67 and 72).

Is Your Office a Clutter Dumping Ground?

Fill in this questionnaire to discover if you are working in a disaster zone.

YES   NO   SOMETIMES

1 Does your heart sink when you enter your workspace because there is so much stuff in it?

2 Is your job suffering because you are working in chaos?

3 Do you constantly suffer from headaches or feel tense that you work in such a mess?

4 If you shut your eyes and imagine your office as a neat, ordered place, does that make you feel better?

5 Is your office full of equipment and paperwork?

If your answer is yes, write below the equipment you have and what sort of paperwork:

❶ _____   **❷** _____
❸ _____   **❹** _____
❺ _____   **❻** _____
❼ _____   **❽** _____
❾ _____   **❿** _____

6 Is your idea of filing stacking piles of paper on the floor?

7 Are you storing equipment that has broken or doesn't work properly?

8 Do you always have an overflowing waste bin?

9 Is your desk so littered with correspondence, files, and notes that you never know where to start work?

If your answer is yes, write down below what is on your desk at the moment:

❶ _____   **❷** _____
❸ _____   **❹** _____
❺ _____   **❻** _____
❼ _____   **❽** _____
❾ _____   **❿** _____

10 Do you try and leave your desk clear each evening?

11 If someone rings with a correspondence query, does it take you ages to find the relevant letter?

12 Do you have a regular weekly/monthly system for paying invoices?

13 Are you always tripping over piles of files and books around your desk?

If your answer is yes, write down what is surrounding your desk at the moment:

❶ _____   **❷** _____
❸ _____   **❹** _____
❺ _____   **❻** _____
❼ _____   **❽** _____
❾ _____   **❿** _____

14 Are you struggling to find current contact numbers because there are so many crossings out in your personal organizer?

15 Are your filing cabinets bulging with too much old material?

If your answer is yes, write down what sort of files they contain (current or redundant):

YES NO SOMETIMES

❶ _____   ❷ _____
❸ _____   ❹ _____
❺ _____   ❻ _____
❼ _____   ❽ _____
❾ _____   ❿ _____

16 Does your computer take ages to download files because the hard disk is too crowded?

17 Do you keep over 100 emails regularly in your inbox?

18 Are there programs on your computer that are out of date or that you never use?

If your answer is yes, list what they are:

❶ _____   ❷ _____
❸ _____   ❹ _____
❺ _____   ❻ _____
❼ _____   ❽ _____
❾ _____   ❿ _____

19 Is your office bulletin or pinboard full of out-of-date cards and contact numbers?

20 Do you have a stationery cupboard/drawer full of unused paper or broken or discarded equipment?

If your answer is yes, list what is in there:

❶ _____   ❷ _____
❸ _____   ❹ _____
❺ _____   ❻ _____
❼ _____   ❽ _____
❾ _____   ❿ _____

21 Do you keep lots of old reference books and magazines on your shelves?

22 Are you still storing accounts material from over fifteen years ago?

23 Is your printer malfunctioning, but you can never be bothered to get it fixed?

24 Do you have a "pending" file or inbox tray that rarely gets looked at?

25 Have you noticed that new work has dwindled since your office became messy?

TOTAL SCORE

Score two points for a "Yes", one for a "Sometimes", and zero for a "No."

35–50
Your office space is becoming out of control – and its disorder is affecting how you perform and your credibility in the workplace. Assess the worst areas to tackle and start on The Home Office project steps (see pages 42–47) to bring the creativity back into your business life.

20–34
You are not buried under paperwork yet, but it is accumulating rapidly, so set up some processing systems before you lose the battle. Deal with your clutter black spots and follow the Home Office project steps (see pages 42–47).

19 and under
Before you start to feel smug at your low score, remember clutter problems can easily sneak up on you. Re-organize any potential clutter hot-spots, and work through any relevant steps in The Home Office project (see pages 42–47).

The Home Office

Draw a plan of your home office as below, showing how your piles of clutter are affecting its flow of chi (see also pages 67 and 72).

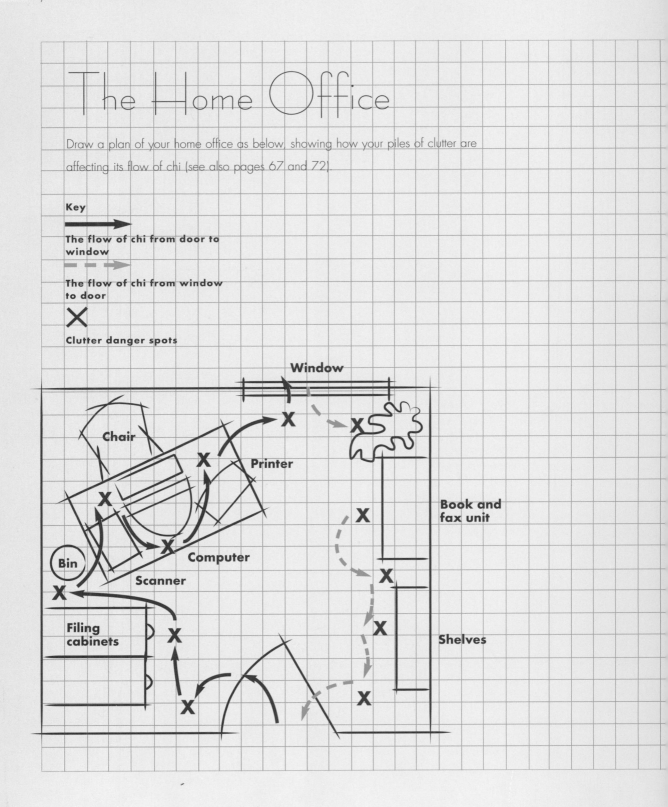

Key

→ **The flow of chi from door to window**

⇢ **The flow of chi from window to door**

✕ **Clutter danger spots**

Window

Chair

Printer

✕

Book and fax unit

Bin

Computer

Scanner

Filing cabinets

Shelves

Your home office plan

Is Your Yard/Garden a Total Mess?

Fill in this questionnaire to find out if your yard or garden is a chaotic mess.

YES   NO   SOMETIMES

1 Is the path leading to your door covered in moss, and are there broken slabs?

2 Do you struggle to reach your door because of the overgrown bushes and shrubs?

3 Does your heart sink as you walk into your chaotic yard or garden?

4 Visualize your perfect space with neat lawns, barbecue area, and florishing borders – does that make you feel good?

5 Is your garden a dumping ground for unwanted goods?

If your answer is yes, detail what junk you have in your garden:

1 _____ **2** _____

3 _____ **4** _____

5 _____ **6** _____

7 _____ **8** _____

9 _____ **10** _____

6 Are your frightened to enter your overcrowded shed?

If your answer is yes, write down the major items in your shed:

1 _____ **2** _____

3 _____ **4** _____

5 _____ **6** _____

7 _____ **8** _____

9 _____ **10** _____

7 Do your garden tools have layers of rust?

8 Are you ashamed to invite people into your yard or garden?

9 When you look out on your front and back spaces, are they choking with weeds?

10 Do you let the grass grow up to knee height before you think of cutting it?

11 Are many parts of your yard or garden broken or decaying?

If your answer is yes, write down what they are:

1 _____ **2** _____

3 _____ **4** _____

5 _____ **6** _____

7 _____ **8** _____

9 _____ **10** _____

12 Do you never invite friends to a barbecue because your back space is an eyesore?

13 Do your drains constantly get blocked up?

14 Do you have lots of cracked terra-cotta pots stacked up out the back?

15 Do you feel insecure because the fence between your house and your neighbors' is falling down?

16 Do you still have builders' debris left from months or years ago?

YES   NO   SOMETIMES

17 If you have a pond, has it been neglected?

If your answer is yes, write down what it now contains:

1 _____ **2** _____

3 _____ **4** _____

5 _____ **6** _____

7 _____ **8** _____

9 _____ **10** _____

18 Have your plants or vegetables been badly attacked by garden pests?

19 Do you regularly dump old fridges, washing machines, or other equipment in your yard or garden?

20 Have you lost your garden hose or is your watering can broken?

21 Do you often leave dead flowers unattended, or have piles of dead leaves around?

22 Is much of your garden furniture broken, badly stained, or unusable?

If your answer is yes, detail what is wrong with it:

1 _____ **2** _____

3 _____ **4** _____

5 _____ **6** _____

7 _____ **8** _____

9 _____ **10** _____

23 Do tradespeople keep complaining to you about your broken gate?

24 Are you always planning to work on the yard or garden, but never seem to make a start?

25 Do you have any rotting or decaying trees?

TOTAL SCORE

Score two points for a "Yes", one for a "Sometimes", and zero for a "No."

35–50
You are in danger of not finding the way into your yard or garden or beating the path to your shed. You will drain your energy and could become discouraged if you leave the area like this, so make a list of your priority hot spots to deal with and start on the Yard/Garden projects' steps on pages 48–59 to restore some harmony and balance in this bountiful space.

20–34
Your yard or garden is not a complete mess of weeds or decaying vegetation, but it is well on its way. Nip it in the bud by working on your worst areas; go through the Yard/Garden steps on pages 48–59.

19 and under
Praise yourself for your low score, but don't become complacent. Your yard or garden may seem a haven now, but a few rainy days can turn it into a jungle – so attend to your worst spots and complete any of the appropriate steps in the Yard/Garden projects on pages 48–59.

The Front Yard and Backyard/Garden

Draw in plans of both your front yard and backyard or garden. For each plan, in the same way as the attic, just draw one chi flow from the door going around the yard in a circular route until it exits via the same door (see page 72). Mark in all clutter, including overgrown shrubs, weeds, decaying trees, stagnant ponds, and broken flowerpots.

Key

The flow of chi from door to window

The flow of chi from window to door

Clutter danger spots

Your front yard/garden plan

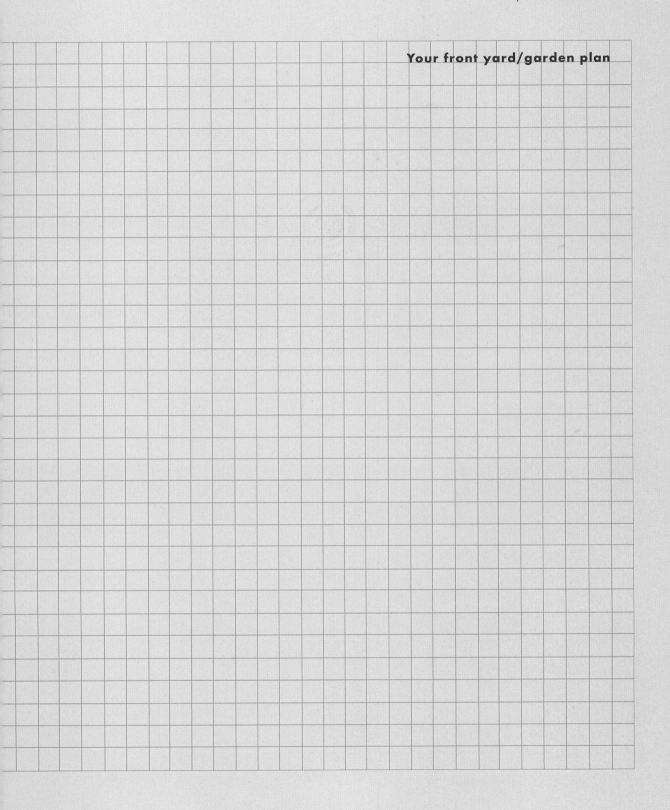